The Ultimate Guide to Cooking Lentils the Indian Way

How To Cook Everything In A Jiffy, Volume 4

Prasenjeet Kumar

Published by Cooking In A Jiffy, 2020.

* Includes INSTANT POT support for over 20 recipes

* Suggests quantities in cups as well as grams and oz

* Recommends minimum salt seasoning in terms of teaspoons

* Suggests adjusting the chilli/heat levels as per taste

Edited By: Arun Kumar Ph.D.

To economize on costs, this book contains no photographs. However, if you wish to know how the dishes actually look, you could either refer to the e-Book version or to the Author's website www.cookinginajiffy.com.

As per Amazon's Kindle match book program, you are entitled to a FREE copy of the Kindle edition of this book when you buy this print version.

Table of Contents

Disclaimers and other information

ALTHOUGH THE AUTHOR has made every effort to ensure that the information in this book was correct at press time, the Author does not assume and hereby disclaims any liability to any party for any loss, damage, or disruption caused by errors or omissions, whether such errors or omissions result from negligence, accident, or any other cause.

This book is not intended as a substitute for the medical advice of physicians. The reader should regularly consult a physician in matters relating to his/her health, and particularly with respect to any symptoms that may require diagnosis or medical attention.

This book also assumes that the reader does not suffer from any food allergies or related medical conditions. Readers suffering from food allergies are requested to skip the recipes that contain ingredients which trigger adverse reactions in that reader or in his/her family and friends.

Acknowledgement

I DEDICATE THIS BOOK to my dearest mom, who is the original creator of all these recipes. It is simply amazing how she, despite being a working mother (she was actually a very senior Indian Administrative Service officer), finds time to not only cook but also experiment with food.

In her quest for experimenting with cooking, she has had the full support of my father (another senior Indian Administrative Service officer) and me.

Most fathers generally leave their wives to cook while they watch television or go out to play golf. While my father did both, he had no hesitation jumping in the kitchen if he thought my mother needed an extra helping hand.

The overall aim used to be to cook meals from scratch within 30 minutes, and it was amazing how often we succeeded in meeting this target.

I, therefore, dedicate this book to my father too, who even now takes time off to "advise" me on what my books should focus on, and sometimes even gives editing suggestions.

"A wise man acts always with reason, and prepares his own lentils himself."

Zeno, the Eastern Roman Emperor

I: Lentils: Why Bother?

OKAY, SO IF YOU WERE a sailor in the 2nd century B.C., with no idea of when exactly could you hit the next dock or port, you certainly had no option but to stock on cereals and legumes/lentils.

You could, of course, carry some fresh fruits and vegetables, and even meat, when you set sail, but in those days of non-refrigerated travel, you had to consume these within 3-5 days.

And then go back to what else, but legumes/lentils.

You could catch fish, but there was no guarantee that you could catch one just in time for your lunch or dinner.

So legumes/lentils were generally what would save your ***.

So much so that the Romans named their emperors after the most common legumes: Lentulus (lentil), Fabius (fava), Piso (pea), and Cicero (chickpea).

A lentil diet was considered necessary in Ancient Rome to achieve a modest temper (as Pliny wrote). Ancient Romans associated lentils with prudent virtues.

But that was then.

Why bother now, when anyone who can eat meat doesn't have to worry about any protein deficiency. Fish, lamb, chicken, turkey, pork, beef, eggs... are all known to be protein-rich foods.

So much so that in the West, if you are a vegetarian or a vegan, a commonly asked question would be:

Don't you run short of proteins if you simply survive on soups and salads?

You may not like the faked, solicitous tone that usually accompanies this query.

But let's face it. The question is quite justified.

Soups and salads may not be sufficient for your daily protein requirement even though it really depends on what you put in your soups and salads.

So, what can a vegetarian or a vegan really do if she doesn't want to become protein deficient?

A cavalier answer would be: go for protein shakes or supplements.

But as I have already discussed in some detail in my book *Healthy Cooking In A Jiffy*, these come in such bewildering forms that, without expert help or supervision, they may cause more harm than good, with terrible side-effects that range from mood swings to gout and kidney stones.

So what natural vegetarian sources of proteins can you then access?

Tofu and nuts immediately come up as worthy options that are rich in proteins and suitable for vegetarians. But that couldn't be the end of the list, could it?

If you want a short answer, then here it is.

Legumes and Lentils.

Yes, you read it correctly.

In ancient times, legumes/lentils were regarded as "a poor man's meat". Now thanks to scientists and expert bodies like the Mayo Clinic, we know that legumes/lentils are not only high in protein, like meats, but are actually better than meat with more dietary fiber and lower fat content.

Adults generally need 10 to 35 percent of their total daily calories from proteins. This amounts to about 50-175 grams of protein a day based on a 2,000-calorie-a-day diet (according to Mayo Clinic).

As per the U.S. Department of Agriculture National Nutrient Database for Standard Reference, 1 cup of cooked legumes/lentils contains over 17 grams of protein. So with some clever permutations and combinations, it should be possible to get all your protein needs from legumes, lentils, and dairy products.

Meat eaters, however, will point out that since legumes/lentils do not contain all nine essential amino acids, they can't, therefore, be regarded as a complete source of proteins. (Tip: They basically lack the amino acids methionine and cysteine.)

The good news, however, is that you can easily get all nine amino acids by consuming legumes/lentils with a grain such as rice.

It is no wonder that Indian home food is considered incomplete without *chawal, dal aur roti* or rice, lentil curry, and Indian bread, respectively. That's probably why Indian cuisine has such a robust tradition of cooking legumes and lentils in a variety of forms that is unmatched by any other cuisine on Planet Earth.

Now I understand how ancient Indians were able to deal with the problem of protein deficiency amongst a population that was forced to remain vegetarian most of the time. The trick was to include a cup of lentil curry (locally known as *dal*) for at least two meals: lunch and dinner.

Make it three if you live in South India!

Other Health Benefits of legumes and lentils also regarded as the "Healthiest Food in the World"

Legumes and lentils are rich in fiber: If you are looking for ways to reduce constipation, relax; you need not swallow anti-constipation pills or those disgusting fiber supplements. Try legumes and lentils instead, which are high in dietary fiber, both soluble and insoluble. Not only do they add bulk to stool, but they have also been found to reduce symptoms of the dreaded Irritable Bowel Syndrome (IBS).

Legumes and lentils are good for a Healthy Heart: It has been found that societies that consume legumes and lentils as part of their regular diet are 82% less at a risk of developing cardiovascular diseases than those who do not. Legumes and lentils contain significant amount of folate and magnesium which do wonders for your heart. Magnesium is considered to be "Nature's Own Channel Blocker". This means that your arteries and veins breathe a sigh of relief as this mineral improves the flow of blood, oxygen, and other nutrients throughout your body.

Legumes and lentils replenish Iron Needed for Energy: Legumes and lentils are rich in iron. Iron is an integral component of hemoglobin, which transports oxygen from the lungs to all body cells. Iron is also a vital component of energy production and metabolism in the body. No wonder, legumes and lentils are nowadays recommended to pregnant women who may be at a risk of iron deficiency, as also to growing children and adolescents in need of iron.

Legumes and lentils are low in cholesterol: Legumes and lentils are preferred over red meat (another rich source of iron) because legumes and lentils, unlike red meat, are low in fat, calories and cholesterol. They are also somewhat lower in oxalic acid and similar chemicals which cause stone formation in kidneys and result in gout, a painful affliction of joints caused by the deposition of oxalate crystals.

Have I now provided enough justification for incorporating legumes and lentils in your diet?

II: Some Interesting Facts about Legumes and Lentils That You May Not Know

LEGUMES AND LENTILS were probably forgotten in the "developed world" with easy availability of red meat and the rise of fast-food joints.

But going back in history, legumes and lentils seem to have been cultivated and consumed for thousands of years, starting from the time of the Neolithic agriculturists.

Archaeologists have found remains of legumes and lentils in the ruins of early farming villages dating back to 7000 B.C. in what is now known as modern day Turkey, Syria, Iraq, and Iran.

Legumes/lentils are mentioned in religious books such as the Bible, Quran and the Vedas. In a Biblical tale, lentils were a godsend to the famished Esau.

The Quran mentions that legumes were vital to the diet of the Christian community in Egypt.

Lentils are consumed during Lent, a time of fasting before Easter, in many Catholic countries. Probably the name "lent" comes from the Latin word "lens" meaning lentils.

Vedas tell us that men domesticated cattle and grew barley, rice, and lentils.

Lentils have been uncovered in tombs and in the underground stores of the pyramids in Egypt. Egypt was known to be the leading seller of lentils in the ancient world.

Ancient Roman writer Pliny reported that a ship left the banks of the Nile with its hold filled with 2,800,000 pounds of lentils destined for Italy.

Ancient Greeks gave up eating lentils when they gained wealth and status. "Now that he is rich he will no longer eat lentils; formerly when he was poor, he ate what he could get," Aristophanes once wrote.

The most interesting fact is legumes and lentils did not always have a good image. They produce gas and sometimes upset stomach. No wonder, legumes and lentils were considered to "bring nightmares and inflame the stomach" in Medieval Europe.

(**Courtesy:** Joel Denker[1])

---

1. http://www.foodpassages.com/jottings-by-joel/intowner-columns/

   the-poor-mans-meat/

III: The Robust Legume/Lentil Cooking Tradition In India

NOW IF YOU ARE CONVINCED that legumes and lentils are good for you and wish to incorporate these in your diet, how should you go about doing that?

After extensive research, I realize that most Westerners have legumes and lentils mostly in their soup.

Forgive me if I sound condescending!

But this attitude seems to flow from the 19th century assumption that legumes and lentils are only good for the poor and are of little nutritional value otherwise. They could, therefore, be had as soups, purees, with toasts and other such inconsequential dishes, as remarked by writer Ella Kellogg once.

At the most, some books would recommend baking legumes and lentils with cheese, putting them in hamburgers, having them with sausages and casseroles, or making lentils stew.

Then you have the famous students' dorm dish of baked beans (straight from the can) and the West Asian "sauce" hummus, without which no Israeli, Lebanese, or Palestinian meal can be termed complete.

I must admit that there is nothing wrong if you want to have your legumes and lentils this way.

But if you want to experiment, and wish to embark upon a roller coaster culinary adventure, you may want to look at Indian cuisine.

If you are an Indian, you need no introduction to this topic.

This is because Indians appear to have adapted and innovated recipes over hundreds or perhaps thousands of years that include legumes/lentils as the MAIN ingredient. The diversity of lentil recipes in India is simply breath taking and even mind boggling at times.

Here are some ways (other than soups or curries!) that legumes and lentils are cooked in India:

Legumes and lentils cooked with rice. Yes, there are many dishes where legumes and lentils are cooked like this.

Recipes include Pea *Pulao* (or rice stir fried with peas), *Khichdi* (a very common dish consumed during various Hindu festivals), *Khichdi's* South Indian variation *Pongal* or *Bisi Bele Bhath*, and its sweet version Sweet *Pongal*. And finally as *Dosas* (rice and lentil pancakes) and *Idlis* (steamed rice and lentil cakes) in the whole of South India.

Legumes and lentils in snacks and accompaniments: You may have heard of Indian snacks called *Pakoras, Khandvi, Dhokhla, Vadas, Madhur Vadas, and Dahi Vadas.*

These are all different kinds of fried or steamed dumplings and fritters, some sweet and others savory. All of them require legumes/lentils as their main ingredient.

Legumes and lentils as Kebabs: This seems to be a pretty recent innovation. So if you are a vegetarian and have perhaps never tried kebabs that your non-vegetarian friends relish with such obvious joy, don't worry, I may have a solution.

Try making these exotic lentil kebab dishes. Believe me, your meat-loving friends too will find these dishes scrumptious. Some of these recipes are so good that your non-vegetarian friends may not be able to differentiate between a meat kebab and its lentil lookalike *Hara Bhara Kebab*.

Legumes and lentils stuffed in breads: Again, you may have heard about the famous Indian *Paratha*. These *ghee* roasted breads come in various sizes and shapes and also differ a bit from region to region. You can stuff these with all kinds of things like potatoes, or cauliflower. However, in the Eastern Indian state of Bihar, there is a tradition of stuffing these *Parathas* with peas, or roasted chickpea flour (also known as *Sattu*), or Split Chick Peas (*Chana Dal*).

It is said that without carrying *Sattu* or roasted chickpea flour with them, for sustenance on those long and arduous treks, Buddhist monks from Bihar could NOT have spread Buddhism to far off places from Afghanistan and Tibet to China, Korea, and Japan!

Legumes and lentils as desserts: Yuck! This may be your first reaction. After all, legumes/lentils are supposed to be bland and flavorless. How can anyone possibly think of having these as desserts?

Let Indian cuisine then disabuse your mind.

Just try *besan* (Chickpea flour) or *Moong Dal* (Bengal Gram) *Halwa* or the famous *motichoor laddoos*, and you would know what I'm talking about.

Still don't believe in India's robust legume/lentil tradition?

Browse through then some of the recipes in the following pages to find out for yourself.

IV: Using Instant Pots

WHEN THIS BOOK WAS originally published, Instant Pots had not become as popular as they are now. Now even the Indian market is full of them with some especially designed for Indian cooking (with a designated button for *Dal*, for example!).

So, when we started getting requests from readers for adding directions for using Instant Pot, we listened. That's why we came out with this new edition where we have adapted over twenty recipes which could be cooked using an Instant Pot.

Please note that not all recipes, in our opinion, can be handled well in an Instant Pot. Especially the ones requiring deep frying, or continuous stirring, or roasting (all recipes in Chapters 3 (Pakoras), 4 (Kebabs), 5 (Parathas) & 6 (Desserts)) – which all can be better tackled the conventional way.

Readers are, however, free to experiment and adapt the recipes as they deem fit.

Chapter 1: The Indian Dal

CALL THEM SOUPS OR curries, but you will find *dals* in almost every home in India.

Vir Sanghvi[1], the noted Indian columnist and gourmand, calls *"Dals the great unifier of India".*

Dals are spiced or tempered in as many ways as there are regions and languages in India. But the common thread would be that, as sources of excellent vegetarian protein, they should be on every Indian's platter.

Vir Sanghvi explains that when *"you talk to foreigners about Indian food, you run into all kinds of misconceptions about what constitutes the essence of Indian cuisine. When I was studying abroad, I was forever being asked, "Do you miss curry?" These days it is more likely to be "Longing for a bit of tandoori chicken, eh?"*

In reality, I've never met an Indian who thinks of his own cuisine in terms of tandoori chicken, a restaurant dish that we rarely eat at home. Nor do I know many Indians who stay awake at nights, when they are away from home, pining for rogan josh or chicken shahi korma or any other kind of curry.

What we do miss is something that foreigners rarely understand.

We miss dal.

---

1. http://www.virsanghvi.com/Article-Details.aspx?key=586

I know grown men who get dal cravings when they have been away from India for long stretches. At University, I knew students who missed the taste of home-cooked dal. And even now, if you ask most Indians what it is that constitutes the heart of real Indian food (the kind that Mummy makes) the answer is nearly always framed in terms of dal."

Touché. I couldn't agree more. These were exactly my thoughts when I was studying law for four years in University College London.

A word of warning though. Most *dals* necessitate the use of Pressure Cookers (or Instant Pots) if you want to cook them in a jiffy.

However, if you do not have a pressure cooker/Instant Pot, you can still cook *dals* in deep sauce pans.

This is how most of rural India and wayside eateries still cook their legumes and lentils, but that does take a much, much longer time.

You will just need to put in slightly more water than suggested for the pressure cooker/Instant Pot based recipes given below.

You will also have to check the *dals* once in a while, while they are cooking, to see whether they have become soft and cooked to your liking. This is also required if you want your *dal* to be thicker, as it is served in popular eateries in India.

Cooking *dals* in Slow Cookers is also possible. Many claim that this method turns out the tastiest of *dals*.

So Pressure Cooker, Instant Pot, Deep Sauce Pan, or Slow Cooker, which ever be your weapon of choice, you can never go wrong with the recipes given below.

Tip: Pre-soaking some *dals* overnight will help reduce their cooking time.

In this backdrop, I shall now present the twenty most popular "Home Style" dal (and curry) recipes, using *Arhar/Toor Dal* (Split Pigeon Peas), *Chana Dal* (Split Chickpea), *Masoor Dal* (Red Lentils), *Moong Dal* (Bengal Gram), *Urad Dal* (Whole/ Split Black Lentils), *Mattar* (Green Peas), *Chhola* (Whole Chickpea), Soya chunks, and *Rajma* (Red Kidney Beans).

Arhar Dal (Split Pigeon Peas)

INGREDIENTS

Arhar/Toor (Split Pigeon Peas) *Dal*-1/2 Small cup (approx. 100 grams or 3.5 oz.)

Water-4 small cups (same cup as above!)

Turmeric (*Haldi*) powder-1/2 tea spoon

Salt– 1/2 tea spoon or to taste

Tomato– 1

Cumin seeds (*Jeera*) – 1/2 tea spoon

Ghee (clarified butter)-1 tea spoon

Fresh Coriander (*Dhania*) leaves (optional)

Method using a Pressure Cooker

Wash the *Arhar Dal* well in a vessel 3-4 times and put it in the pressure cooker with water, turmeric, salt, and chopped tomato.

Close the lid with weight, put it on your heat source, and let it come to full pressure (i.e. when the weight lifts and there is a whistling sound).

Thereafter reduce the heat to minimum (to *Sim* on a gas stove), and let it cook for 5 more minutes.

Turn the gas off, and let the cooker cool down.

Take a tempering pan, add the *ghee,* and put it on your heat source.

When the ghee warms up, add the cumin seeds, and let these splutter. Please ensure that the cumin doesn't burn and only turns brown.

Add this to the *dal.*

Your simple *Arhar Dal* is ready.

If you want, you may add some chopped fresh coriander leaves and serve.

Prep time: 5 minutes for washing and collecting all ingredients

Cooking time: 12 minutes for cooking with pressure cooker.

Total time: 17 minutes

Method using an Instant Pot

Wash the *Arhar Dal* well in a vessel 3-4 times.

Turn on the Instant Pot.

Press the Sauté button and take it to high.

Add the ghee in the inner pot.

When the ghee warms up, add the cumin seeds, and let these splutter. Please ensure that the cumin doesn't burn and only turns brown.

Now add the washed *Arhar Dal,* and put it in the Instant Pot with water, turmeric, salt, and chopped tomato.

Close the lid, and pressure cook for six minutes. Let it cool down naturally.

Your simple *Arhar Dal* is ready.

If you want, you may add some chopped fresh coriander leaves and serve.

Prep time: 5 minutes for washing and collecting all ingredients

Cooking time: 10 minutes with Instant Pot.

Total time: 15 minutes

Note: Different Instant Pot models may have different designs or control options, so please feel free to adapt as you deem fit.

Arhar Dal (Variation with rai, onion, garlic and curry leaves)

THE WESTERN INDIAN states of Gujarat and Maharashtra prefer to cook their *Arhar/Toor dal* with this tasty twist, where they use black mustard seed (*Rai*) and curry leaves in place of cumin (*Jeera*) and coriander leaves. Do try this out.

Ingredients

Arhar/Toor (Split Pigeon Peas) *Dal*-1/2 Small cup (approx. 100 grams or 3.5 oz.)

Water-4 small cups (same cup as above!)

Turmeric (*Haldi*) powder-1/2 tea spoon

Salt– 1/2 tea spoon or to taste

Tomato– 2

Onion-1

Garlic-4 pieces

Rai (Black Mustard seed whole) – 1/2 tea spoon

Curry leaves-few

Ghee (clarified butter)-2 tea spoon

Method using a Pressure Cooker

Wash the *Arhar Dal,* and put it in the pressure cooker with water, turmeric, salt, and chopped tomatoes, onion, and garlic.

Close the lid with weight, put it on your heat source, and let it come to full pressure (i.e. when the weight lifts and there is a whistling sound).

Thereafter reduce the heat to minimum (to *Sim* on a gas stove), and let it cook for 5 more minutes.

Turn the heat source off, and let the cooker cool down.

Take a tempering pan, add the *ghee,* and put it on your heat source.

When the *ghee* warms up, add the *rai* till it splutters, and then add the curry leaves.

Please ensure that the *rai* doesn't burn.

Add this to the *dal.*

Your simple *Arhar Dal* variation is ready.

Prep time: 5 minutes for washing and collecting all ingredients

Cooking time: 12 minutes for cooking with pressure cooker

Total time: 17 minutes

Method using an Instant Pot

Wash the *Arhar Dal*.

Turn on the Instant Pot.

Press the Sauté button and take it to high.

Add the *ghee* in the inner pot.

When the *ghee* warms up, add the *rai* till it splutters, and then add the curry leaves.

Please ensure that the *rai* doesn't burn.

Now add the washed *Arhar Dal,* and put it in the Instant Pot with water, turmeric, salt, and chopped tomato, onion and garlic.

Close the lid, and pressure cook for six minutes.

Let it cool down naturally.

Your *Arhar Dal* variation is ready.

Prep time: 5 minutes for washing and collecting all ingredients

Cooking time: 10 minutes with Instant Pot.

Total time: 15 minutes

Note: Different Instant Pot models may have different designs or control options, so please feel free to adapt as you deem fit.

Chana Dal (Split Chickpea)

———

THIS IS ONE OF THOSE rare *dals* which is cooked with *garam masala*. This makes it go well with *pulao* or even meat dishes that are cooked with *garam masala*.

Ingredients

Chana Dal (Split Chickpea)-1/2 cup (approx. 100 grams or 3.5 oz.)

Water-4 cups (same cup as above!)

Turmeric (*Haldi*) powder-1/2 tea spoon

Salt– 1/2 tea spoon or to taste

Tomato– 2

Onion-1

Garlic-2 pieces

Ginger-1 inch

Cumin seeds (*Jeera*) – 1/2 tea spoon

Garam Masala (mixture of common Indian spices) crushed -1/2 tea spoon

Tip: If you can't get ready-made *garam masala* mixture from a nearby Indian store, you can make yours by using 1 black

cardamom, 3 green cardamoms, 4 cloves, and 1 inch cinnamon-all ground together for this dish.

Ghee (clarified butter)-2 tea spoon

Method using a Pressure Cooker

Wash the *Chana Dal.*

Put the pressure cooker on your heat source, and add *ghee* (Clarified butter).

When the *ghee* heats up, add the cumin seeds for browning.

Add the chopped-up onion, garlic, and ginger.

Sauté for 2 minutes.

Add the tomatoes, and sauté for another minute.

Add the *dal*, turmeric, salt, water, and *garam masala.*

Close the lid, and let it come to full pressure (i.e. when the weight lifts and there is a whistling sound).

Reduce heat (to Sim on a gas stove), and let it cook for 10 more minutes.

Turn off the heat source, and let the cooker cool down.

Your simple *Chana dal* is ready.

Prep time: 5 minutes for washing and collecting all ingredients

Cooking time: 15 minutes with pressure cooker

Total time: 20 minutes

Method using an Instant Pot

Wash the *Chana Dal*.

Turn on the Instant Pot.

Press the Sauté button, and take it to high.

Add the ghee in the inner pot.

When the *ghee* heats up, add the cumin seeds for browning.

Add the chopped up onion, garlic, and ginger.

Sauté for 2 minutes.

Add the tomatoes, and sauté for another minute.

Add the *dal*, turmeric, salt, water, and *garam masala*.

Close the lid, and let the Instant Pot pressure cook for 10 minutes.

Let the Instant Pot cool down naturally.

Your simple *Chana dal* is ready.

Prep time: 5 minutes for washing and collecting all ingredients

Cooking time: 15 minutes with Instant Pot

Total time: 20 minutes

Note: Different Instant Pot models may have different designs or control options, so please feel free to adapt as you deem fit.

Chana Dal (Split Chickpea) - Bihari style

THIS *dal* is a complete side dish that goes well with *puris* and *pulaos*.

Ingredients

Chana Dal (Split Chickpea)-1/2 cup (approx. 100 grams or 3.5 oz.)

Water-3 cups (same cup as above!)

Turmeric (*Haldi*) powder-1/2 tea spoon

Salt– 1/2 tea spoon or to taste

Sugar- ¼ tea spoon

Desiccated coconut- 2 tea spoons

Tomato– 2

Onion-1

Garlic-2 pieces

Ginger-1 inch

Cumin seeds (*Jeera*) – 1/2 tea spoon

Garam Masala (mixture of common Indian spices) crushed -1/ 2 tea spoon

Tip: If you can't get ready-made *garam masala* mixture from a nearby Indian store, you can make yours by using 1 black cardamom, 3 green cardamoms, 4 cloves, and 1 inch cinnamon-all ground together for this dish.

Asafoetida (*Hing*) - ½ tea spoon

Ghee (clarified butter)-2 tea spoon

Method using a Pressure Cooker

Wash the *Chana Dal*.

Put the pressure cooker on your heat source, and add *ghee* (Clarified butter).

When the *ghee* heats up, add the cumin seeds for browning.

Add the chopped up onion, garlic, and ginger.

Sauté for 2 minutes.

Add the tomatoes, and sauté for another minute.

Now add the coconut, asafoetida (*Hing*) and stir well.

Add the dal, turmeric, salt, sugar, water, and *garam masala*.

Close the lid, and let it come to full pressure (i.e. when the weight lifts and there is a whistling sound).

Reduce heat (to Sim on a gas stove), and let it cook for 10 more minutes.

Turn off the heat source, and let the cooker cool down.

Your *Chana dal-* Bihari style is ready.

Prep time: 5 minutes for washing and collecting all ingredients

Cooking time: 15 minutes with pressure cooker

Total time: 20 minutes

Method using an Instant Pot

Wash the *Chana Dal*.

Turn on the Instant Pot.

Press the Sauté button, and take it to high.

Add the ghee in the inner pot.

When the *ghee* heats up, add the cumin seeds for browning.

Add the chopped up onion, garlic, and ginger.

Sauté for 2 minutes.

Add the tomatoes, and sauté for another minute.

Now add the coconut and asafoetida (*Hing*), and stir well.

Add the dal, turmeric, salt, sugar, water, and *garam masala*.

Close the lid, and let the Instant Pot pressure cook for 10 minutes.

Let the Instant Pot cool down naturally.

Your *Chana dal-* Bihari style is ready.

Prep time: 5 minutes for washing and collecting all ingredients

Cooking time: 15 minutes with Instant Pot

Total time: 20 minutes

Note: Different Instant Pot models may have different designs or control options, so please feel free to adapt as you deem fit.

Masoor Dal (Whole Red Lentils)

INGREDIENTS

Whole *Masoor Dal*-1/2 cup (approx. 100 grams or 3.5 oz.)

Water-4 cups (same cup as above!)

Turmeric (*Haldi*) powder-1/2 tea spoon

Salt– 1/2 tea spoon or to taste

Tomato– 2

Onion-1

Garlic-2 pieces

Cumin seeds (*Jeera*) – 1/2 tea spoon

Ghee (clarified butter)-2 tea spoon

Method using a Pressure Cooker

Wash the *Masoor Dal.*

Put the cooker on your heat source, and add *ghee* (Clarified butter).

When the *ghee* heats up, add the cumin seeds for browning.

Add the chopped up onion and garlic.

Sauté for 2 minutes.

Add the tomatoes, and sauté some more for another minute.

Add the *dal*, turmeric, salt, and water.

Close the lid, and let it come to full pressure (i.e. when the weight lifts, and there is a whistling sound).

Reduce the heat (to SIM on a gas stove), and let it cook for 10 minutes.

Turn off the heat source, and let the cooker cool down.

Your simple *Masoor dal* is ready.

Prep time: 5 minutes for washing and collecting all ingredients

Cooking time: 13 minutes with pressure cooker

Total time: 18 minutes

Method using an Instant Pot

Wash the *Masoor Dal*.

Turn on the Instant Pot.

Press the Sauté button, and take it to high.

Add the ghee in the inner pot.

When the *ghee* heats up, add the cumin seeds for browning.

Add the chopped up onion and garlic.

Sauté for 2 minutes.

Add the tomatoes, and sauté some more for another minute.

Add the *dal*, turmeric, salt, and water.

Close the lid, and let the Instant Pot pressure cook for 10 minutes.

Let the Instant Pot cool down naturally.

Your simple *Masoor dal* is ready.

Prep time: 5 minutes for washing and collecting all ingredients

Cooking time: 13 minutes with Instant Pot

Total time: 18 minutes

Note: Different Instant Pot models may have different designs or control options, so please feel free to adapt as you deem fit.

Dhuli Masoor Dal (Split Red Lentils)

Dhuli Masoor (Split Red Lentils) *Dal*-1/2 cup (approx. 100 grams or 3.5 oz.)

Water-4 cups

Turmeric (*Haldi*) powder-1/2 teaspoon

Salt– 1/2 teaspoon or to taste

Tomato– 2

Cumin seeds (*Jeera*) – 1/2 tea spoon

Garlic-4 cloves

Whole Red Chilli-1 (just for flavor and not to make it hot; you can add more if you like it hot)

Cooking Oil-1 tea spoon

Fresh Coriander (optional)

Method using a Pressure Cooker

Wash the *Masoor Dal,* and put it in the pressure cooker with water, *haldi*, salt, and chopped tomato.

Close the lid with weight, put it on your heat source, and let it come to full pressure (i.e. when the weight lifts, and there is a whistling sound).

Thereafter switch off the heat source, and let the cooker cool down.

Take a tempering pan, add the cooking oil, and put it on your heat source.

When it warms up, add the cumin seeds and whole red chilli, and let it splutter. Please ensure that the cumin doesn't burn and only turns brown.

Add the garlic, and let it roast for a few seconds till it starts giving off a lovely aroma.

Add this to the *dal*.

Your simple *Dhuli Masoor Dal* is ready.

If you want, you may add some chopped fresh coriander leaves to it and serve.

Prep time: 5 minutes for washing and collecting all ingredients

Cooking time: 7 minutes with pressure cooker

Total time: 12 minutes

Method using an Instant Pot

Wash the *Masoor Dal*

Turn on the Instant Pot.

Press the Sauté button and take it to high.

Add the ghee in the inner pot.

When the ghee warms up, add the cumin seeds and whole red chilli and let it splutter. Please ensure that the cumin doesn't burn and only turns brown.

Add the garlic, and let it roast for a few seconds till it starts giving off a lovely aroma.

Now add the washed *Masoor Dal,* and put it in the Instant Pot with water, *haldi*, salt, and chopped tomato.

Close the lid and pressure cook for 5 minutes.

Let the Instant Pot cool naturally.

Your simple *Dhuli Masoor Dal* is ready.

If you want, you may add some chopped fresh coriander leaves to it and serve.

Prep time: 5 minutes for washing and collecting all ingredients

Cooking time: 5 minutes with Instant Pot

Total time: 10 minutes

Note: Different Instant Pot models may have different designs or control options, so please feel free to adapt as you deem fit.

Pachmahal Dal (Mixture of five lentils)

INGREDIENTS

Arhar Dal - 1 tablespoon

Dhuli Moong - 1 tablespoon

Dhuli Masoor Dal- 1 tablespoon

Chana Dal - 1 tablespoon

Split *Urad Dal* - 1 tablespoon

Water-4 cups

Turmeric (*Haldi*) powder-1/2 tea spoon

Salt– 1/2 tea spoon or to taste

Tomato– 2

Onion-1

Garlic-4 pieces

Cumin seeds (*Jeera*) – 1/2 tea spoon

Ghee (clarified butter)-2 tea spoon

Method using a Pressure Cooker

Mix and wash all the *Dals* together.

Put the cooker on your heat source, and add *ghee* (Clarified butter).

When the *ghee* heats up, add the cumin seeds for browning.

Add the chopped up onion and garlic.

Sauté for 2 minutes.

Add the tomatoes, and sauté some more for another minute.

Add the *dal*, turmeric, salt, and water.

Close the lid, and let it come to full pressure (i.e. when the weight lifts, and there is a whistling sound).

Reduce the heat (to SIM on a gas stove) and let it cook for 10 minutes.

Turn off the heat source, and let the cooker cool down.

Your *Pachmahal dal* is ready.

Prep time: 5 minutes for washing and collecting all ingredients

Cooking time: 13 minutes with pressure cooker

Total time: 18 minutes

Method using an Instant Pot

Mix and wash all the *Dals* together.

Turn on the Instant Pot.

Press the Sauté button, and take it to high.

Add the ghee in the inner pot.

When the *ghee* heats up, add the cumin seeds for browning.

Add the chopped up onion and garlic.

Sauté for 2 minutes.

Add the tomatoes, and sauté some more for another minute.

Add the *dals*, turmeric, salt, and water.

Close the lid, and let the Instant Pot pressure cook for 10 minutes.

Let the Instant Pot cool down naturally.

Your *Pachmahal dal* is ready.

Prep time: 5 minutes for washing and collecting all ingredients

Cooking time: 13 minutes with Instant Pot

Total time: 18 minutes

Note: Different Instant Pot models may have different designs or control options, so please feel free to adapt as you deem fit.

Dhuli Moong Dal (Split Bengal gram)

INGREDIENTS

Dhuli Moong (Split Bengal Gram) *Dal*-1/2 cup (approx. 100 grams or 3.5 oz.)

Water-4 cups (same cup as above!)

Turmeric (*Haldi*) powder-1/2 tea spoon

Salt– 1/2 tea spoon or to taste

Tomato– 1

Cumin seeds (*Jeera*) – 1/2 tea spoon

Ghee (clarified butter)-1 tea spoon

Fresh Coriander (optional)

Method using a Pressure Cooker

Wash the *Moong Dal* and put it in the pressure cooker with water, *haldi*, salt, and chopped tomato.

Close the lid with weight, put it on your heat source, and let it come to full pressure (i.e. when the weight lifts, and there is a whistling sound).

Thereafter switch off the heat source, and let the cooker cool down.

Take a tempering pan, add the ghee and put it on your heat source.

When it warms up, add the cumin, and let it splutter.

Please ensure that the cumin doesn't burn and only turns brown.

Add this to the *dal*.

Your simple *Moong Dal* is ready.

If you want, you may add some chopped fresh coriander leaves to it and serve.

Prep time: 5 minutes for washing and collecting all ingredients

Cooking time: 7 minutes with pressure cooker

Total time: 12 minutes

Method using an Instant Pot

Wash the *Moong Dal*.

Turn on the Instant Pot.

Press the Sauté button, and take it to high.

Add the ghee in the inner pot.

When the ghee warms up, add the cumin seeds, and let these splutter. Please ensure that the cumin doesn't burn and only turns brown.

Now add the washed *Moong Dal,* and put it in the Instant Pot with water, *haldi*, salt, and chopped tomato.

Close the lid, and pressure cook for three minutes. Let it cool down naturally.

Your simple *Moong Dal* is ready.

If you want, you may add some chopped fresh coriander leaves to it and serve.

Prep time: 5 minutes for washing and collecting all ingredients

Cooking time: 4 minutes with Instant Pot

Total time: 9 minutes

Note: Different Instant Pot models may have different designs or control options, so please feel free to adapt as you deem fit.

Moong Dal Dhuli (Split Bengal Gram): Bengali style

INGREDIENTS

Dhuli Moong (Split Bengal Gram) *Dal*-1/2 cup (approx. 100 grams or 3.5 oz.)

Water-4 cups (same cup as above!)

Turmeric (*Haldi*) powder-1/2 tea spoon

Salt– 1/2 tea spoon or to taste

Sugar- ¼ tea spoon

Desiccated coconut - 2 tea spoons

Garam Masala- ½ tea spoon

Tip: If you can't get ready-made *garam masala* mixture from a nearby Indian store, you can make yours by using 1 black cardamom, 3 green cardamoms, 4 cloves, and 1 inch cinnamon-all ground together for this dish.

Tomato—2

Onion (chopped) - 1

Garlic (chopped) – 2 cloves

Ginger (chopped) - 1 inch (2.5 cm or 1/3rd length of a finger) piece

Cumin seeds (*Jeera*) – 1/2 tea spoon

Ghee (clarified butter)-2 tea spoons

Fresh Coriander (optional)

Method using a Pressure Cooker

Take the *Moong Dal,* and put it in a pan, **without washing**.

Put the pan on the heat source, and dry roast the *Moong Dal* till it turns a nice golden brown color.

Switch off the heat source. Now wash the *Moong Dal,* and keep it aside. (The Moong Dal will not roast properly if you have washed it and made it wet. That's why you have to roast the Moong Dal first and then wash it.)

In a pressure cooker, add the *ghee,* and put it on your heat source.

As soon as the *ghee* warms up, add the cumin seeds.

Let it splutter which takes a few seconds only. Please ensure that the cumin doesn't burn and only turns brown.

Now add the onion, garlic, and ginger and stir till the onions become translucent.

Now add the *Moong Dal* (roasted and washed), desiccated coconut, *garam masala*, sugar, turmeric, salt, tomato, and water.

Close the lid with weight, put it on your heat source, and let it come to full pressure (i.e. when the weight lifts, and there is a whistling sound).

Thereafter switch off the heat source, and let the cooker cool down.

Your *Moong Dal*-Bengali style is ready.

If you want, you may add some chopped fresh coriander leaves to it and serve.

Prep time: 7 minutes for washing and collecting all ingredients

Cooking time: 5 minutes with pressure cooker

Total time: 12 minutes

Method using an Instant Pot

Turn on the Instant Pot.

Press the Sauté button, and take it to high.

Take the *Moong Dal,* and put it in the Instant Pot, **without washing**.

Dry roast the *Moong Dal* till it turns a nice golden brown color.

Switch off the Instant Pot.

Remove the *Moong Dal, wash it* and keep it aside. (The Moong Dal will not roast properly if you have washed it and made it wet. That's why you have to roast the Moong Dal first and then wash it.)

Again turn on the Instant Pot.

Press the Sauté button, and take it to high.

Add the ghee in the inner pot.

As soon as the *ghee* warms up, add the cumin seeds.

Let it splutter which takes a few seconds only. Please ensure that the cumin doesn't burn and only turns brown.

Now add the onion, garlic, and ginger and stir till the onions become translucent.

Now add the *Moong Dal* (roasted and washed), desiccated coconut, *garam masala*, sugar, turmeric, salt, tomato, and water.

Close the lid, and pressure cook for three minutes.

Let it cool down naturally. Your *Moong Dal*-Bengali style is ready.

If you want, you may add some chopped fresh coriander leaves to it and serve.

Prep time: 7 minutes for washing and collecting all ingredients

Cooking time: 5 minutes with Instant Pot

Total time: 12 minutes

Note: Different Instant Pot models may have different designs or control options, so please feel free to adapt as you deem fit.

Split Urad Dal (Black Lentils) with Spinach

INGREDIENTS

Split *Urad Dal*- 1/2 cup (approx. 100 grams or 3.5 oz.)

Water-3 cups (same cup as above!)

Spinach- 2 cups (washed and chopped) (approx. 200 grams or 7 oz.)

Ginger-1 inch (2.5 cm or 1/3rd length of a finger) piece

Cumin seeds- ½ tea spoon

Fresh tomatoes-3

Ghee (clarified butter) - 1 table spoon

Salt– 1/2 tea spoon or to taste

Method using a Pressure Cooker

In a pan, dry roast the *Urad Dal* till it turns golden brown.

Now wash the dal and keep it aside.

In a pressure cooker, add the *ghee,* and put it on your heat source.

As soon as the *ghee* melts, add the cumin seeds and ginger.

As soon as the cumin seeds brown, add the spinach, and the tomatoes.

Stir well.

Now add the *Urad dal*, salt, and water.

Close the lid of the cooker with weight.

Once it comes to full pressure, (i.e. when the weight lifts, and there is a whistling sound), turn down the flame (to SIM on a gas stove), and let it cook for 15 minutes.

Switch off the heat source, and once the cooker cools down, take out the *dal*.

Your *Urad*-Spinach *dal* is ready.

Prep time: 7 minutes

Cooking time: 15 minutes

Total time: 22 minutes

Method using an Instant Pot

Turn on the Instant Pot.

Press the Sauté button, and take it to high.

Take the *Urad Dal,* and put it in the inner pot without washing.

Dry roast the *Urad Dal* till it turns golden brown.

Switch off the Instant Pot.

Now wash the dal, and keep it aside.

In the Instant Pot, press the Sauté button, and take it to high.

Add the *ghee* in the inner pot.

As soon as the *ghee* warms up, add the cumin seeds and ginger.

As soon as the cumin seeds brown, add the spinach and the tomatoes.

Stir well.

Now add the *Urad dal*, salt, and water.

Close the lid, and pressure cook for five minutes.

Let it cool down naturally.

Your *Urad*-Spinach *dal* is ready.

Prep time: 7 minutes

Cooking time: 10 minutes

Total time: 17 minutes

Note: Different Instant Pot models may have different designs or control options, so please feel free to adapt as you deem fit.

Sambar

THE SOUTH INDIAN STATES of Andhra Pradesh, Tamil Nadu, Karnataka, and Kerala prefer to cook their *Arhar/Toor dal* with this fiery but tasty twist. In fact, they love *Sambar* so much that they have to have it for all meals– breakfast, lunch and dinner!

Be careful, this is NOT a mild lentil soup.

Ingredients

Arhar/Toor (Split Pigeon Peas) *Dal*-1 small cup (approx. 200 grams or 7 oz.)

Water-4 cups (same cup as above!)

Onion-1

Tomatoes-2

Garlic-6 cloves

Beans-100 grams (3.5oz) (half cup)

Pumpkin-100 grams (3.5oz) (half cup)

Bottle Gourd-100 grams (3.5oz) (half cup)

Sambar masala powder-4 teaspoon

Tip: If you can't get ready-mix Sambar masala powder from a nearby store or find it too spicy, you can make yours by mixing together: 1 teaspoon *Chana Dal* (Split Chickpea), 1 teaspoon *Urad Dal* (Black Lentils), 1 tablespoon *Dhania* (whole coriander) seeds, ½ teaspoon *Kali Mirch* (black pepper corns), ½ teaspoon *Methi* (fenugreek) seeds, ½ teaspoon *Hing* (Asafoetida), 1 teaspoon *Jeera* (cumin seeds), 1 dry red chilli whole (if you don't mind the heat!), and dry roasting them for a minute. Grind (in a mixie-grinder) and store in an airtight jar.

Tamarind paste-1 tablespoon dissolved in 1/2 cup of water

Ghee-1 tablespoon

Black Mustard seeds (*Rai*)-1 teaspoon

Curry leaves-10-12

Salt– 1/2 tea spoon or to taste

Sugar-1/2 teaspoon

Method using a Pressure Cooker

Wash the *dal* and vegetables well.

Chop up the vegetables, onion, tomatoes, and garlic.

In a pressure cooker, put the *dal* and the chopped vegetables along with the chopped onion, tomatoes, and garlic.

Add the *sambar* masala, salt, and sugar.

Add water.

Close the lid, and put it on your heat source.

When the pressure cooker comes to full pressure (i.e. when the weight lifts and there is a whistling sound), reduce the heat (to SIM on a gas stove), and let it cook for 7 minutes.

Let the cooker cool down on its own and then open it.

Add the tamarind paste and boil it once more without covering it with the lid.

In a tempering pan, add the *ghee*, the black mustard seeds, and the curry leaves, and put it on your heat source.

When the seeds splutter, add this mixture to the *Sambar*.

That's all. Your *Sambar* is ready.

In case, you cannot get curry leaves, black mustard seeds alone can also impart the required flavor.

If you like your *Sambar* to taste sourer, you can add more tamarind paste. Similarly, if you want your *Sambar* to taste sweeter, you can add more sugar.

Prep time: 8 minutes for washing, chopping, and collecting all ingredients

Cooking time: 12 minutes with pressure cooker

Total time: 20 minutes

Method using an Instant Pot

Wash the *dal* and vegetables well.

Chop up the vegetables, onion, tomatoes, and garlic.

Turn on the Instant Pot.

Press the Sauté button, and take it to high.

Add the ghee in the inner pot.

When the ghee warms up, add the black mustard seeds, and the curry leaves. Let the seeds splutter.

Now add the *dal* and the chopped vegetables along with the chopped onion, tomatoes, and garlic.

Add the *sambar* masala, salt, and sugar.

Add water.

Close the lid, and pressure cook for ten minutes. Let it cool down naturally.

When the Instant Pot has cooled down, open the lid, and add the tamarind paste.

Press the Sauté button, and boil it once more without covering it with the lid.

That's all. Your *Sambar* is ready.

In case, you cannot get curry leaves, black mustard seeds alone can also impart the required flavor.

If you like your *Sambar* to taste sourer, you can add more tamarind paste. Similarly, if you want your *Sambar* to taste sweeter, you can add more sugar.

Prep time: 8 minutes for washing, chopping and collecting all ingredients

Cooking time: 12 minutes with Instant Pot

Total time: 20 minutes

Note: Different Instant Pot models may have different designs or control options, so please feel free to adapt as you deem fit.

Legumes and lentils as Curries

LET ME NOW PRESENT you legumes and lentils, which are not made like *dals*, but as proper curries. They, therefore, don't look like soups at all!

Rajma (Red Kidney Beans curry)

A PERENNIAL FAVORITE of the North Indian states of Punjab, Haryana, Himachal Pradesh and Jammu & Kashmir, this dish is cooked more like meat than lentils. Many wayside eateries or *dhabas* thrive on serving just *Rajma* with fragrant Basmati rice and readily find a seemingly never ending queue of diners.

Try this dish once and you will not touch that can of insipid Baked Beans with tomato sauce ever again!

Ingredients

Red Kidney beans (*Rajma*)-1 small cup (approx. 100 grams or 3.5 oz.)

Water-4 cups (same cup as above!)

Chopped Onion-1

Chopped Garlic-5 cloves

Chopped Ginger-1 inch (2.5 cm or 1/3rd length of a finger) piece

Chopped Tomatoes-4

Garam Masala powder-1/2 teaspoon

Tip: If you can't get ready-made *garam masala* mixture from a nearby Indian store, you can make yours by using 1 black

cardamom, 3 green cardamoms, 4 cloves, and 1 inch cinnamon-all ground together for this dish.

Turmeric (*Haldi*)-1/2 teaspoon

Cumin seeds (*Jeera*)-1/2 teaspoon

Kashmiri red chilli powder-1/2 teaspoon (just for flavor and not to make it hot; you can add more if you like it hot)

Clarified butter (*Ghee*)-2 tablespoon

Salt– 1/2 tea spoon or to taste

Sugar-1/4 teaspoon

Method using a Pressure Cooker

Soak the kidney beans overnight in 2 cups of water.

Note: Remember if you don't pre-soak the beans, the cooking time will be extremely long, and the beans may not cook that easily.

Place the pressure cooker on your heat source.

Add the clarified butter, and when it melts, add the cumin seeds.

As soon as the cumin seeds turn brown, which takes just a few seconds (do please make sure they don't burn), add the chopped onion, garlic, and ginger.

Sauté well till the onions become translucent and start giving off a nice aroma.

Add the kidney beans, along with the chilli powder, turmeric powder, *garam masala*, salt, and sugar.

Sauté for about a minute.

To this mixture, now add the tomatoes.

Roast well till the tomatoes are cooked.

Now add 4 cups of water and close the lid.

Let the cooker come to full pressure i.e. when steam starts escaping from the vent (don't worry, you will hear that typical sound), and then immediately reduce the heat to minimum.

In other words, if cooking on gas, turn the knob to SIM (mer).

Cook on low heat for 15 minutes more.

Thereafter turn off the heat source, and let the cooker cool on its own.

Open the lid and see if the *Rajma* has the desired consistency. In case you want it to be more wettish, you can add some more water. In case you want it drier, then you can put it back on the heat source without the lid, and let the excess water evaporate. While doing either, please remember to keep stirring, so that the *Rajma* does not burn.

This dish tastes delicious with plain, long grain Basmati rice.

Prep time: Soak overnight. After that prep time should be about 5 minutes for washing and collecting all ingredients.

Cooking time: 20 minutes with pressure cooker

Total time: 25 minutes

Method using an Instant Pot

Soak the kidney beans overnight in 2 cups of water.

Note: Remember if you don't pre-soak the beans, the cooking time will be extremely long and the beans may not cook that easily.

Turn on the Instant Pot.

Press the Sauté button, and take it to high.

Add the ghee in the inner pot and when it warms up, add the cumin seeds.

As soon as the cumin seeds turn brown, which takes just a few seconds (do please make sure they don't burn), add the chopped onion, garlic, and ginger.

Sauté well till the onions become translucent and start giving off a nice aroma.

Add the kidney beans, along with the chilli powder, turmeric powder, *garam masala*, salt, and sugar.

Sauté for about a minute.

To this mixture, now add the tomatoes.

Roast well till the tomatoes are cooked.

Now add 4 cups of water, close the lid, and pressure cook for thirty minutes. Let it cool down naturally.

Alternatively, you can press the chilli bean button on your Instant Pot, if there is one.

Open the lid and see if the *Rajma* has the desired consistency. In case you want it to be more wet, you can add some more water. In case you want it drier, then you can put it back on Sauté without the lid and let the excess water evaporate. While doing either, please remember to keep stirring, so that the *Rajma* does not burn.

This dish tastes delicious with plain, long grain Basmati rice.

Prep time: Soak overnight. After that prep time should be about 5 minutes for washing and collecting all ingredients.

Cooking time: 35 minutes with Instant Pot

Total time: 40 minutes

Note: Different Instant Pot models may have different designs or control options, so please feel free to adapt as you deem fit.

Chhola (Whole Chickpea Curry)

THIS IS ANOTHER CLASSIC dish of the North Indian states of Punjab, Haryana, Himachal Pradesh and Jammu & Kashmir. Again, like *Rajma*, this dish too is cooked more like meat than lentils. However, unlike *Rajma* which is traditionally enjoyed with fragrant Basmati rice, *Chhola* is paired more with *Pooris* (fried and puffed up Indian unleavened bread) and *Bhathuras* (another variation of fried and puffed up Indian leavened bread). This combo is in fact quite a *favorite* for breakfasts or rather brunches.

Try this dish with rice or any kind of bread, Western or Indian, and I bet you will fall in love with it.

Ingredients

Whole white Chickpea (*Kabuli Chana* or *Chhola*)-1 small cup (approx. 200 grams or 7 oz.)

Onions-2

Garlic-6 cloves

Ginger-1+1/2 inches (4 cm or 2/3rd length of a finger) piece

Tomatoes-3

Cumin seeds (*Jeera*)-1/2 teaspoon

Coriander powder-2 teaspoon

Turmeric- 1 teaspoon

Garam Masala powder-1/2 teaspoon

Tip: If you can't get ready-made *garam masala* mixture from a nearby Indian store, you can make yours by using 1 black cardamom, 3 green cardamoms, 4 cloves, and 1 inch cinnamon-all ground together for this dish.

Kashmiri Red Chilli powder-1/2 teaspoon (just for flavor and not to make it hot; you can add more if you like it hot)

Cooking Oil- 2 tablespoon

Salt– 1/2 tea spoon or to taste

Method using a Pressure Cooker

Soak the chickpeas in a vessel with water (which covers the chickpeas completely) at least for 4 hours. This way when you cook the chickpeas, they become nice and tender and take less time to cook.

Put the pre-soaked chickpeas in a pressure cooker, with enough water to cover the chickpeas.

Switch on the heat source, and close the lid of the pressure cooker with weight.

When the cooker comes to full pressure, i.e. when steam starts escaping from the vent (don't worry, you will hear that typical sound), reduce the heat (to Sim on a gas stove), and let the chickpeas cook for 10 minutes more.

Turn off the heat source, and let the cooker cool down.

In a grinder, make a fine paste of the tomatoes, ginger, garlic, and onion.

Place a wok on a heat source, and add the cooking oil.

When the oil warms up, add the cumin seeds.

In a few seconds, as soon as the cumin seeds turn brown, add the paste you have just made in the grinder. Do please ensure that the cumin seeds do not burn.

Sauté the paste till it starts giving off a nice aroma.

Now add the turmeric powder, *garam masala*, red chilli powder, and coriander powder.

Sauté for another 2 minutes.

Now, add the chickpeas (without the water) to this mixture.

Mix well and add the salt.

Then, add as much water as you like depending upon the thickness of the curry that you want.

Let the mixture boil for about 2 minutes so that all the ingredients are well blended.

Your *Chhola* is ready.

Prep time: Soak overnight or at least for 4 hours. After that prep time should be 5 minutes for washing and collecting all ingredients.

Cooking time: 20 minutes with pressure cooker

Total time: 25 minutes

Method using an Instant Pot

Soak the chickpeas in a vessel with water (which covers the chickpeas completely) at least for 4 hours. This way when you cook the chickpeas, they become nice and tender and take less time to cook.

In a grinder, make a fine paste of the tomatoes, ginger, garlic, and onion.

Turn on the Instant Pot.

Press the Sauté button, and take it to high.

Add the cooking oil in the inner pot.

When the oil warms up, add the cumin seeds.

In a few seconds, as soon as the cumin seeds turn brown, add the paste you have just made in the grinder. Do please ensure that the cumin seeds do not burn.

Sauté the paste till it starts giving off a nice aroma.

Now add the turmeric powder, *garam masala*, red chilli powder, coriander powder, and salt.

Sauté for another 2 minutes.

Now add the pre-soaked chickpeas, with enough water to cover the chickpeas. Pressure cook for 30 minutes. Let it cool down naturally.

Alternatively, you can press the chilli bean button on your Instant Pot, if there be one.

In case you want the curry to be more wet, you can add some more water. In case you want it drier, then you can put it back on Sauté without the lid and let the excess water evaporate. While doing either, please remember to keep stirring, so that the chickpea does not burn.

Your *Chhola* is ready.

Prep time: Soak overnight or at least for 4 hours. After that prep time should be 5 minutes for washing and collecting all ingredients.

Cooking time: 35 minutes with Instant Pot

Total time: 40 minutes

Note: Different Instant Pot models may have different designs or control options, so please feel free to adapt as you deem fit.

Note: If you have sampled *Chhola* in a *dhaba* (wayside eatery), you may find my "Home Style" recipe a little mild. This is for two main reasons. First, since the *dhabas* have to cook huge quantities (say 10 Kgs or 22 lbs of chickpeas in one go), and that too in big non-pressurized vessels, they slip in some baking soda to their pre-soaking process. I'm not in favor of this practice because this unnecessarily increases the sodium levels of your *Chhola* (which is bad for your blood pressure) without enhancing the taste. In fact, the somewhat soapy taste that baking soda imparts to this dish may not suit sensitive palates.

Which leads to the second point of drowning this baking soda induced flavor. This is done by using stronger spices like *Kastoori Methi* (fragrant Fenugreek). Then *Anardana* (ground seeds of wild pomegranate) is used to increase the tanginess of the dish. Finally, used tea leaves are added to impart a blackish color to the *Chhola*.

I have nothing against the second or the third points. Use these if you crave the authentic *dhaba* flavor.

But for the first, you may be better off using a pressure cooker or a slow cooker than using baking soda.

Chhola Dry (Whole Chickpea Dry)

THIS IS AN EXCELLENT dish which can be had as a mid-morning or afternoon snack. It is healthy as it is prepared **without using even a drop of oil**.

Ingredients

Whole white Chickpea (*Kabuli Chana* or *Chhola*)-1 small cup (approx. 200 grams or 7 oz.)

Onions-1 (chopped)

Tomatoes-2 (chopped)

Fresh Coriander leaves- 1 tea spoon (chopped)

Deseeded green chilli- 1 (optional) (chopped) (just for flavor and not to make it hot; you can use the seeds if you like it hot)

Fresh Lemon juice- 1 table spoon

Salt– 1/2 tea spoon or to taste

Method using a Pressure Cooker

Soak the chickpeas in a vessel with water (which covers the chickpeas completely) at least for 4 hours. This way when you cook the chickpeas, they become nice and tender and take less time to cook.

Put the pre-soaked chickpeas in a pressure cooker, with enough water to cover the chickpeas. Also add salt.

Switch on the heat source, and close the lid of the pressure cooker with weight.

When the cooker comes to full pressure, i.e. when steam starts escaping from the vent (don't worry, you will hear that typical sound), reduce the heat (to Sim on a gas stove), and let the chickpeas cook for 10 minutes more.

Turn off the heat source, and let the cooker cool down.

Take out the chickpeas (without the water) into a serving bowl.

Add the chopped onion, tomatoes, coriander leaves, green chilli, and lemon juice, and mix well.

Your delicious dry *Chhola* is ready.

Prep time: Soak overnight or at least for 4 hours. After that prep time should be 5 minutes for washing and collecting all ingredients.

Cooking time: 15 minutes with pressure cooker

Total time: 20 minutes

Method using an Instant Pot

Soak the chickpeas in a vessel with water (which covers the chickpeas completely) at least for 4 hours. This way when you cook the chickpeas, they become nice and tender and take less time to cook.

Turn on the Instant Pot.

Put the pre-soaked chickpeas in the inner pot with enough water to cover the chickpeas. Also add salt.

Close the lid and pressure cook for 30 minutes. Let it cool naturally.

Alternatively, you can press the chilli bean button on your Instant Pot, if there be one.

Take out the chickpeas (without the water) into a serving bowl.

Add the chopped onion, tomatoes, coriander leaves, green chilli, and lemon juice, and mix well.

Your delicious dry *Chhola* is ready.

Prep time: Soak overnight or at least for 4 hours. After that prep time should be 5 minutes for washing and collecting all ingredients.

Cooking time: 30 minutes with Instant Pot

Total time: 35 minutes

Note: Different Instant Pot models may have different designs or control options, so please feel free to adapt as you deem fit.

Whole Green Chana Ghugni (Green Chickpea Bihari Style Curry)

INGREDIENTS

Green *Chana (Chickpea)*- ½ cup (approx. 100 grams or 3.5 oz.)

Onion- 1 (chopped)

Tomato- 1 (chopped)

Cumin seeds- ½ tea spoon

Cooking oil- 1 tea spoon

Water- 1 cup

Salt– 1/2 tea spoon or to taste

Method using a Pressure Cooker

Pre-soak the green chickpeas in a vessel with water (which covers the green chickpeas completely) at least for 4 hours. This way when you cook the chickpeas, they become nice and tender and take less time to cook.

Place the pressure cooker on your heat source.

Add the cooking oil, and when it warms up, add the cumin seeds.

As soon as the cumin seeds turn brown, which takes just a few seconds (do please make sure they don't burn), add the chopped onion, and the tomatoes.

Stir well till the onions become translucent and start giving off a nice aroma.

Now add the green *chana*, salt, and the water.

Close the lid of the pressure cooker with weight.

When the cooker comes to full pressure, i.e. when steam starts escaping from the vent (don't worry, you will hear that typical sound), reduce the heat (to Sim on a gas stove), and let the chickpeas cook for 5 minutes more.

Turn off the heat source, and let the cooker cool down.

Your Green *Chana Ghugni* is ready.

Prep time: Soak overnight or at least for 4 hours. After that prep time should be 5 minutes for washing and collecting all ingredients.

Cooking time: 10 minutes with pressure cooker

Total time: 15 minutes

Method using an Instant Pot

Pre-soak the green chickpeas in a vessel with water (which covers the green chick peas completely) at least for 4 hours. This way when you cook the chickpeas, they become nice and tender and take less time to cook.

Turn on the Instant Pot.

Press the Sauté button, and take it to high.

Add the cooking oil in the inner pot.

When the oil warms up, add the cumin seeds.

As soon as the cumin seeds turn brown, which takes just a few seconds (do please make sure they don't burn), add the chopped onion, and the tomatoes.

Stir well till the onions become translucent and start giving off a nice aroma.

Now add the green *chana*, salt, and the water.

Close the lid and pressure cook for 10 minutes.

Alternatively, you can press the chilli bean button on your Instant Pot, if there be one.

Let the Instant Pot cool down naturally.

Your Green *Chana Ghugni* is ready.

Prep time: Soak overnight or at least for 4 hours. After that prep time should be 5 minutes for washing and collecting all ingredients.

Cooking time: 15 minutes with Instant Pot

Total time: 20 minutes

Note: Different Instant Pot models may have different designs or control options, so please feel free to adapt as you deem fit.

Green Peas and Potato Ghugni (Bihari style curry)

THIS IS THE FAVORITE "Railway Station" dish all over North India that is usually served with *Pooris* (fried and puffed up unleavened Indian bread).

Ingredients

Green Peas- ½ cup (approx. 100 grams or 3.5 oz.)

Potato- 1 (cut into bite size pieces)

Tomato- 2 (chopped)

Cumin seeds- ½ tea spoon

Cooking oil- 1 tea spoon

Water- 1/2 cup

Salt– 1/2 tea spoon or to taste

Method using a Pressure Cooker

Place the pressure cooker on your heat source.

Add the cooking oil, and when it warms up, add the cumin seeds.

As soon as the cumin seeds turn brown, which takes just a few seconds (do please make sure they don't burn), add the peas, and the potato.

Stir well for about a minute, and add the tomatoes.

Stir till the tomatoes are slightly cooked.

Now add salt and the water.

Close the lid of the pressure cooker with weight.

When the cooker comes to full pressure, i.e. when steam starts escaping from the vent (don't worry, you will hear that typical sound), turn off the heat source, and let the cooker cool down.

Your Green Pea-Potato *Ghugni* is ready.

Prep time: 5 minutes

Cooking time: 5 minutes with pressure cooker

Total time: 10 minutes

Method using an Instant Pot

Turn on the Instant Pot.

Press the Sauté button, and take it to high.

Add the cooking oil in the inner pot.

When the oil warms up, add the cumin seeds.

As soon as the cumin seeds turn brown, which takes just a few seconds (do please make sure they don't burn), add the peas, and the potato.

Stir well for about a minute, and add the tomatoes.

Stir till the tomatoes are slightly cooked.

Now add salt and the water.

Close the lid and pressure cook for 5 minutes. Let it cool naturally.

Your Green Pea-Potato *Ghugni* is ready.

Prep time: 5 minutes

Cooking time: 5 minutes with Instant Pot

Total time: 10 minutes

Note: Different Instant Pot models may have different designs or control options, so please feel free to adapt as you deem fit.

Green Peas Dal (Bihari style)

———

INGREDIENTS

Green Peas- 1½ cup (approx. 300 grams or 10 oz.)

Tomato- 3 (chopped)

Cumin seeds- ½ tea spoon

Turmeric- ½ tea spoon

Red Chilli powder-1/4 tea spoon (just for flavor and not to make it hot; you can add more if you like it hot)

Garam Masala-½ tea spoon

Tip: If you can't get ready-made *garam masala* mixture from a nearby Indian store, you can make yours by using 1 black cardamom, 3 green cardamoms, 4 cloves, and 1 inch cinnamon-all ground together for this dish.

Coriander powder-1 tea spoon

Ghee (clarified butter) - 1 table spoon

Water- 2 cups

Salt– 1/2 tea spoon or to taste

Method using a Pressure Cooker

In a blender, crush ½ cup green peas, and keep aside.

Place the pressure cooker on your heat source.

Add the *ghee* and when it warms up, add the cumin seeds.

As soon as the cumin seeds turn brown, which takes just a few seconds (do please make sure they don't burn), add the peas, both crushed and whole.

Stir well for about a minute, and add the tomatoes.

Stir till the tomatoes are slightly cooked.

Now add turmeric, coriander, red chilli powder, *garam masala,* and salt.

Stir again for a minute. Add water.

Close the lid of the pressure cooker with weight.

When the cooker comes to full pressure, i.e. when steam starts escaping from the vent (don't worry, you will hear that typical sound), reduce the heat (to Sim on a gas stove), and let the peas cook for 5 minutes more.

Turn off the heat source, and let the cooker cool down.

Your Green Peas *Dal* (Bihari style) is ready.

Prep time: 7 minutes

Cooking time: 10 minutes with pressure cooker

Total time: 17 minutes

Method using an Instant Pot

In a blender, crush ½ cup green peas, and keep aside.

Turn on the Instant Pot.

Press the Sauté button, and take it to high.

Add the *ghee* in the inner pot, and when it warms up, add the cumin seeds.

As soon as the cumin seeds turn brown, which takes just a few seconds (do please make sure they don't burn), add the peas, both crushed and whole.

Stir well for about a minute, and add the tomatoes.

Stir till the tomatoes are slightly cooked.

Now add turmeric, coriander, red chilli powder, *garam masala,* and salt.

Stir again for a minute. Add water.

Close the lid. Pressure cook for 5 minutes. Let it cool down naturally.

Your Green Peas *Dal* (Bihari style) is ready.

Prep time: 7 minutes

Cooking time: 10 minutes with Instant Pot

Total time: 17 minutes

Note: Different Instant Pot models may have different designs or control options, so please feel free to adapt as you deem fit.

Karhi (Yoghurt Chickpea Flour Curry)

THIS DISH WAS PROBABLY invented for those days when you couldn't get any fresh green vegetables in the local village market. That need has more or less disappeared with the arrival of supermarkets that access food from anywhere in the world.

Nonetheless, *Karhi* remains quite popular not only in Northern India but in Western India also, with a little variation.

Note: This recipe, in my opinion, is not suited for Instant Pot as it requires constant stirring.

Here is the Western Indian version, which I find tastier.

Ingredients

Curd (Indian/Greek style yoghurt)-1 cup (approx. 200 grams or 7 oz.)

Chickpea flour (*Besan*)-2 tablespoon

Turmeric powder (*Haldi*)-1 teaspoon

Coriander powder (*Dhania*)-1 teaspoon

Kashmiri Red Chilli powder- ½ teaspoon (just for flavor and not to make it hot; you can add more if you like it hot)

Sugar- 1 teaspoon

Ground Asafoetida (*Hing*)-1/4 teaspoon

Whole green chilli-1 (just for flavor).

If you like your *karhi* to be hot, you can chop the green chilli in small pieces and mix it.

Salt-1 teaspoon or to taste

Water-2 + ½ cups

Clarified butter (*Ghee*) - 1 teaspoon

Black Mustard seeds (*Rai*)-1/2 teaspoon

Curry leaves-few

Method

In a wok or deep sauce pan, mix together the yoghurt, Chickpea flour (*Besan*), Turmeric powder (*Haldi*), Coriander powder, Kashmiri Red Chilli powder, Sugar, Asafoetida (*Hing*), whole green chilli, and salt.

Mix well and then add the water.

Switch on the heat source and place the wok/deep sauce pan on it.

Let the mixture come to a boil, but keep stirring till it gets a nice slightly thick consistency (approximately 5 minutes).

Remove thereafter from the heat source.

Separately, in a tempering pan, add the clarified butter, the black mustard seeds, and the curry leaves, and put it on your heat source.

As soon as the mustard seeds (*rai*) splutter, turn off the heat source, and add the entire contents of the tempering pan to the *Karhi* in the wok/deep sauce pan.

That's all.

This *Karhi* tastes really good with rice.

You can also add *Pakoris* (vegetables, including onions rolled in *besan* and fried; recipes in Chapter 3) to the *Karhi*.

If you prefer the North Indian version of *Karhi*, then leave out the curry leaves and *Rai* from the above recipe.

Prep time: 5 minutes

Cooking time: 7 minutes

Total time: 12 minutes

Mattar Paneer (Cottage Cheese with peas in a curry)

THIS IS THE CLASSIC North Indian dish that you will find everywhere, in homes, *dhabas* as well as fancy restaurants. Here is a low calorie version, however.

Ingredients

Paneer (Cottage cheese) – 500 grams (approx. 18oz or 2 cups)

Green peas (shelled, fresh are preferred) – 200 grams (approx. 7oz or 1 cup)

Medium size Onions– 2

Garlic-4 pieces

Ginger-1 inch (2.5 cm or 1/3rd length of a finger) piece

Fresh tomato-2 (washed and chopped)

Turmeric (*Haldi*) - 1/2 tea spoon

Dry crushed Coriander seeds-2 tea spoon

Garam Masala (mixture of common Indian spices) crushed- 1/2 tea spoon

Tip: If you can't get ready-made *garam masala* mixture from a nearby Indian store, you can make yours by using 1 black

cardamom, 3 green cardamoms, 4 cloves, and 1 inch cinnamon-all ground together for this dish.

Kashmiri Red Chilli powder– 1/4 tea spoon (Recommended for color, but if you like your dish to be really spicy, use some other red chilli powder)

Cumin seeds whole (*Jeera*)-1/2 tea spoon

Salt-1 level tea spoon (or to taste)

Tomato Ketchup-1 table spoon

Cooking oil-1 table spoon

Ghee (clarified butter)-1 tea spoon

Water-1 tea cup

Method using a Pressure Cooker

Take the *Paneer* (cottage cheese) and dry roast it in a non- stick pan till it turns golden brown. It can then be cut into bite size pieces.

(Most recipes would advise that you fry these pieces in oil, which you can, if you don't mind the additional calories.)

Blend together (in a blender preferably!) the onions, garlic, ginger, and tomatoes to a fine paste.

Heat the oil in a pressure cooker. (In case you don't have a pressure cooker, you can use a wok or a deep sauce pan).

Add cumin seeds to the oil, and as it turns brown, add this paste, and gently fry the same.

As the paste starts giving off a nice aroma, add the peas and the cottage cheese, and sauté gently.

Add all the dry *masala* and salt to this mixture.

Add the Ketchup and *Ghee* to the mixture and stir again.

Add the water, close the lid with weight and bring it to full pressure i.e. when steam starts escaping from the vent (don't worry, you will hear that typical sound).

Turn off the heat.

Let the cooker cool down on its own before opening it.

(In case you are using a wok/pan, add the water, cover the wok/pan with a lid and reduce the heat to minimum. Let the peas cook to your liking, which should take about 5 minutes).

Your *Mattar paneer* (cottage cheese with peas curry) is ready.

Prep time: 10 minutes

Cooking time: 5 minutes with pressure cooker, 10 minutes with a wok/pan

Total time: 15 minutes with pressure cooker, 20 minutes with a wok/pan

Method using an Instant Pot

Take the *Paneer* (cottage cheese) and dry roast it in a non- stick pan till it turns golden brown. It can then be cut into bite size pieces.

(Most recipes would advise that you fry these pieces in oil, which you can, if you don't mind the additional calories.)

Blend together (in a blender preferably!) the onions, garlic, ginger and tomatoes to a fine paste.

Turn on the Instant Pot.

Press the Sauté button, and take it to high.

Add the cooking oil in the inner pot.

When the oil warms up, add the cumin seeds and as it turns brown, add the blended paste, and gently fry the same.

As the paste starts giving off a nice aroma, add the peas and the cottage cheese and sauté gently.

Add all the dry *masala* and salt to this mixture.

Add the Ketchup and *Ghee* to the mixture and stir again.

Add the water, close the lid, and pressure cook for 2 minutes.

Your *Mattar paneer* (cottage cheese with peas curry) is ready.

Prep time: 10 minutes

Cooking time: 5 minutes with Instant Pot

Total time: 15 minutes

Note: Different Instant Pot models may have different designs or control options, so please feel free to adapt as you deem fit.

Soya Mattar (Soya Granules-Peas Curry)

INGREDIENTS

Soya Granules—1 cup (approx. 200 grams or 7 oz.)

Green peas (shelled fresh are preferred) –1/2 cup (approx. 100 grams or 3.5 oz.)

Medium size Onions– 2 (chopped)

Garlic-4 pieces

Ginger-1 inch (2.5 cm or 1/3rd length of a finger) piece

Fresh tomato-2 (chopped)

Turmeric (*Haldi*) - 1/2 tea spoon

Dry crushed coriander (*Dhania*) seeds-2 tea spoon

Garam Masala (mixture of common Indian spices) crushed- 1/2 tea spoon

Tip: If you can't get ready-made *garam masala* mixture from a nearby Indian store, you can make yours by using 1 black cardamom, 3 green cardamoms, 4 cloves, and 1 inch cinnamon-all ground together for this dish.

Kashmiri Red Chilli powder– 1/4 tea spoon (Recommended for color, but if you like your dish to be really spicy, use any other red chilli powder)

Curd (Indian/Greek style yoghurt)-1 table spoon

Cumin whole (*Jeera*)-1/2 tea spoon

Salt-1 level tea spoon (or to taste)

Tomato Ketchup-1 table spoon

Cooking oil-1 table spoon

Ghee (clarified butter)-1 tea spoon

Water-1 cup

Method using a Pressure Cooker

Blend together (in a blender preferably!) the onions, garlic, ginger, and tomatoes to a fine paste.

Heat the oil in a pressure cooker/wok/deep pan.

Add cumin to the oil and as it turns brown, add this paste and gently fry the same.

As the paste starts giving off a nice aroma, add the soya granules and peas to it. Sauté gently.

Add all the dry *masala*, salt, and curd to this mixture and keep stirring on low flame (SIM on a gas stove) till it starts becoming dry.

Add the Ketchup to the mixture and stir again.

At this juncture, add the *Ghee* for a lovely flavor.

Add the water, close the lid with weight (in case using a pressure cooker), and bring it to full pressure on high flame i.e. when steam starts escaping from the vent (don't worry, you will hear that typical sound).

Switch off the heat source.

Let the cooker cool down on its own before opening it.

In case you are using a wok/deep pan, cover that with a tight fitting lid and cook for about 15 minutes or till the soya granules are completely cooked.

Prep time: 7 minutes

Cooking time: 10 minutes with pressure cooker; 20 minutes with a wok/deep pan

Total time: 17 minutes with pressure cooker; 27 minutes with a wok/deep pan

Method using an Instant Pot

Blend together (in a blender preferably!) the onions, garlic, ginger, and tomatoes to a fine paste.

Turn on the Instant Pot.

Press the Sauté button and take it to high.

Add the cooking oil in the inner pot.

When the oil warms up, add the cumin seeds and as it turns brown, add the blended paste and gently fry the same.

As the paste starts giving off a nice aroma, add the soya granules and peas to it. Sauté gently.

Add all the dry *masala*, salt, and curd to this mixture and keep stirring till it starts becoming dry.

Add the Ketchup to the mixture and stir again.

At this juncture, add the *Ghee* for a lovely flavor.

Add the water, close the lid, and pressure cook for three minutes. Let the Instant Pot cool naturally.

Prep time: 7 minutes

Cooking time: 10 minutes with Instant Pot

Total time: 17 minutes

Note: Different Instant Pot models may have different designs or control options, so please feel free to adapt as you deem fit.

Dal Makhni

THIS IS THE MOST POPULAR "lentil with tomato" dish that you can get from wayside eateries to gourmet deluxe restaurants throughout India. Traditionally, this *dal* is slow cooked overnight and so is considered very tedious for cooking at home. Also it is more of a dairy product with one restaurant recipe suggesting the use of half a kilo (1 lb. approx.) of cream and a full kilo of butter for each kg of *dal*!

We, therefore, dare to present a lower calorie and a JIFFYier version.

Ingredients

Whole *Urad Dal* (Black Lentils) -1/2 cup (approx. 100 grams or 3.5 oz.) (soaked overnight)

Water-5 cups

Garlic-2 pieces

Ginger-1 inch (2.5 cm or 1/3rd length of a finger) piece

Fresh tomatoes-3

Tomato puree- 200 grams (1 cup or 7 oz.)

Fresh low-fat cream-200 grams (1 cup or 7 oz.)

Butter salted-25 grams (1 + 1/2 tablespoon)

Salt-to taste (or 1 level teaspoon roughly)

Sugar-1/2 tea spoon

Method using a Pressure Cooker

Wash the *dal* and put it in the cooker.

Add Garlic and ginger crushed together with the fresh tomatoes and the tomato puree.

Add the salt, sugar, and water.

Light the flame and close the lid of the cooker. Once it comes to full pressure i.e. when steam starts escaping from the vent (don't worry, you will hear that typical sound), turn down the flame to SIM, and let it cook for 30 minutes.

Switch off the heat source and once the cooker cools down, add the butter and low-fat cream to the *dal*.

Bring it to boil once without the lid.

Your low calorie *dal makhni* is ready in a jiffy.

Prep time: 7 minutes

Cooking time: 40 minutes

Total time: 47 minutes

Method using an Instant Pot

Wash the *dal* and put it in the inner pot.

Add garlic and ginger crushed together with the fresh tomatoes and the tomato puree.

Add the salt, sugar, and water.

Close the lid and turn on the Instant Pot. Pressure cook for 30 minutes. Let it cool naturally.

Open the lid and press the Sauté button.

Add the butter and the low-fat cream.

Bring it to a boil.

Your low calorie *dal makhni* is ready in a jiffy.

Prep time: 7 minutes

Cooking time: 40 minutes

Total time: 47 minutes

Note 1: Different Instant Pot models may have different designs or control options, so please feel free to adapt as you deem fit.

Note 2: This recipe will taste like the famous *Dal Bukhara* served by a 5-star Hotel in Delhi.

However, if you long for the *Dal Makhni* prepared by restaurants like the *Moti Mahal,* you will have to then use two other legumes and lentils viz. *Rajma* (red kidney beans) and *Chana Dal* (Split Chickpea) along with the *Urad Dal* (black lentils) used in this recipe. The proportions would be: *Urad: Rajma:Chana::* 1: ½: ½.

For a fascinating discussion on the origins of this famous *Dal*, please refer to Vir Sanghvi's "The modern dal makhani was invented by Moti Mahal[1]".

---

1. http://www.virsanghvi.com/Article-Details.aspx?key=451

Chapter 2: Legumes and Lentils Cooked With Rice

DAL IS SO MUCH a symbol of India that almost every cuisine that came into contact with Indian cooking was charmed into incorporating lentils into its food. For example, when the Zoroastrian Parsis first fled to India, in the 7th and 8th centuries, they encountered *dal* which was not a staple in their native Iran. So they invented their own unique dishes that had chunks of meat made with lentils resulting into the famous *dhansak*.

The Mughals were equally enthusiastic in experimenting with *dal*, which they were otherwise unfamiliar with in Samarkand, or wherever they came from in Central Asia. As Vir Sanghvi postulates:

"In the 16th and 17th centuries, the staple food of Indian peasants was kitchdi, made with dal and rice (or sometimes, millets). The Mughals, who were used to the pulaos of Central Asia, were unfamiliar with the idea of cooking rice with dal. They fell in love with kitchdi and in the 15 years that Humayun spent in exile, his Indian cooks made kitchdi for his guests, including the Shah of Iran. Jehangir was so fond of Gujarati kitchdi that he ate it regularly in his palace."

But *Khichdi* is not the only famous dish that has rice cooked along with lentils. You have its South Indian cousin of *Pongal* and its sweeter version of Sweet *Pongal*. Then you have the famous *Dosas* and *Idlis*.

I, therefore, start by cataloguing the Home Style versions of six such famous combo dishes of rice cooked with legumes and lentils.

Mattar Pulao (Peas Rice)

INGREDIENTS

Long grain rice (Basmati)-1 cup (approx. 200 grams or 7 oz.)

Peas-1/2 cup (approx. 100 grams or 3.5 oz.)

Sliced Onion-1 (Medium)

Water-2 cups

Cumin seeds (*Jeera*)-1/2 teaspoon

Green Cardamom (*Chhoti elaichi*)-2

Cinnamon (*Dalchini*)-1/2 inch

Cloves (*Laung*)-4

Bay leaf (*Tejpatta*)-1

Clarified butter (*Ghee*)-2 tablespoon

Salt– 1/2 tea spoon or to taste

Sugar-1/4 teaspoon

Method

Wash the rice well (in a vessel 3-4 times, but don't rub it lest the grains break) and let it "dry" naturally, on an inclined plate, for 15-20 minutes. This helps enhance the aroma.

If using a pressure cooker:

In a pressure cooker, add the clarified butter, and place it on your heat source.

When the butter warms up, add the cumin seeds along with the cardamom, cinnamon, cloves, and bay leaves.

As soon as it all starts giving off a nice aroma, in less than a minute, add the onion slices and fry till translucent.

Do please make sure that the spices brown and not burn, otherwise your dish will be ruined.

Add the peas, and stir for a minute.

Now add the rice along with the salt and sugar.

Stir well.

Add the water.

Close the lid of the pressure cooker, BUT remove the weight.

When steam starts escaping from the vent, reduce the heat to minimum.

In other words, if cooking on gas, turn the knob to SIM (mer).

Wait for 10 minutes, and switch off the gas.

Take out the rice. Your Pea *Pulao* is ready.

If using a thick bottomed pan/vessel:

In a pan/vessel, add the clarified butter, and place it on your source of heat.

When the butter warms up, add the cumin seeds along with the cardamom, cinnamon, cloves, and bay leaves.

As soon as it all starts giving off a nice aroma, which should be in less than a minute, add the onion slices and fry till translucent.

Do please make sure that the spices brown and not burn, otherwise your dish will be ruined.

Add the peas, and stir for a minute.

Now add the rice along with the salt and sugar.

Stir well.

Add the water.

Cover the pan/vessel with a well-fitting lid.

Reduce the heat to minimum.

In other words, if cooking on gas, turn the knob to SIM (mer).

Let the rice cook for 15-20 minutes.

Switch off the heat source and let the rice remain in the vessel for another 5 minutes.

Take out the rice. Your pea *pulao* is ready.

Prep time: 20 minutes

Cooking time: 12 minutes with a pressure cooker; 17-22 minutes with a deep pan

Total time: 32 minutes with a pressure cooker; 37-42 minutes with a deep pan

If using an Instant Pot:

Wash the rice well (in a vessel 3-4 times, but don't rub it lest the grains break) and let it "dry" naturally, on an inclined plate, for 15-20 minutes. This helps enhance the aroma.

Turn on the Instant Pot.

Press the Sauté button, and take it to high.

Add ghee in the inner pot.

When the ghee warms up, add the cumin seeds along with the cardamom, cinnamon, cloves, and bay leaves.

As soon as it all starts giving off a nice aroma, in less than a minute, add the onion slices and fry till translucent.

Do please make sure that the spices brown and not burn, otherwise your dish will be ruined.

Add the peas and stir for a minute.

Now add the rice along with the salt and sugar.

Stir well.

Add the water.

Close the lid and press the rice button. Otherwise pressure cook for 5 minutes. And let it cool naturally.

Take out the rice. Your Pea *Pulao* is ready.

Prep time: 7 minutes

Cooking time: 10 minutes with Instant Pot

Total time: 17 minutes

Note: Different Instant Pot models may have different designs or control options, so please feel free to adapt as you deem fit.

Khichdi (Mixture Dish of Rice, Lentil and Veggie)

KHICHDI literally means a mixture. In some form or another, this is almost compulsorily prepared for the festival of *Makar Sakranti* that is celebrated all over India and Nepal. This festival is also known as *Pongal* in Tamil Nadu, *Bihu* in Assam, *Lohri* in Punjab, or *Uttarayan* in Gujarat.

Interestingly, this is one of the few Hindu festivals that falls on the fixed day of 14 January, when the Sun moves from the Tropic of Capricorn to the Tropic of Cancer heralding the arrival of spring and the beginning of the harvest season.

It is believed that on this day, Lord Surya (the Sun God) visits the house of his son *Shani* (Saturn), who is the lord of the *Makar rashi* (Capricorn) and the controller of the quantum of misfortune befalling humans. To appease *Shani*, therefore, many Indians prefer cooking *Khichdi* on Saturdays which is also known as *Shaniwar* or the day of Lord *Shani*.

Khichdi is otherwise the most nutritionally complete dish, consisting of carbs from rice, proteins from legumes and lentils, and vitamins from veggies. Also it is quite a JIFFY dish.

Ingredients

Rice-3/4 cup (approx. 150 grams or 5 oz.)

Moong Dal (Split Bengal Gram)-1/4 cup (approx. 50 grams or 1.75 oz.)

Onion-1 (chopped up)

Ginger-1 inch (2.5 cm or 1/3rd length of a finger) piece

Spinach (only leaves)-500 grams or 18oz or 2 cups coarsely chopped

Peas– 100 grams (half cup or 3.5 oz)

Carrots-2 (cut into small pieces)

Tomato-1

Khada (that is, whole and not powdered) *Garam Masala* (Green cardamom– 2, brown cardamom-1, Bay leaves-2, cinnamon stick-1/2 inch, black pepper-6, cloves-4, cumin seeds-1/2 tea spoon)

Coriander (*Dhania*) powder-1 teaspoon

Red chilli powder (only for flavor and not to make it hot)-1/4 teaspoon (you can add more if you like it hot)

Turmeric (*Haldi*)-1 teaspoon

Asafoetida (*Hing*)-1/4 teaspoon

Ghee (clarified butter)-2 tablespoon full

Salt- 1 level teaspoon roughly or to taste.

Water-3 cups (This will give your *Khichdi* a wet consistency. However, if you like your *Khichdi* to be drier, then add only 2 cups of water instead of 3.)

Method

Wash the rice and *dal* together and let it dry for 5 minutes on an inclined plate.

If using a pressure cooker:

In a pressure cooker, put the clarified butter, and put it on your heat source.

As it warms up, add the *Khada Garam Masala* and Asafoetida.

Let these all crackle but NOT burn.

Now add the onion and ginger.

Sauté this for 2 minutes, and then add the peas and the carrots.

Stir well.

Now add the coarsely chopped spinach, turmeric, coriander powder, red chilli powder, and salt.

Add the rice, *dal,* and the tomatoes.

Stir well.

Add the water, and put the lid with the weight on the cooker.

After the cooker comes to full pressure, i.e. when steam starts escaping from the vent (don't worry, you will hear that typical sound), switch off the heat source but do NOT release the pressure.

Let the pressure cooker cool down by itself.

Open the cooker and you will find your *Khichdi* ready.

If using a thick bottomed pan/vessel:

In a pan/vessel, add the clarified butter and place it on your heat source.

When the butter warms up, add the *Khada Garam Masala* and Asafoetida (*Hing*).

Let these all crackle but NOT burn.

Now add the onion and ginger.

Sauté this for 2 minutes.

Then add the peas and the carrots.

Stir well.

Then add the coarsely chopped spinach, turmeric, coriander powder, red chilli powder, and salt.

Add the rice, *dal,* and the tomatoes.

Stir well.

Add the water.

Cover the pan/vessel with a well-fitting lid.

Reduce the heat to minimum.

In other words, if cooking on gas, turn the knob to SIM (mer).

Let the *Khichdi* cook for 15-20 minutes.

Switch off the heat source, and let the rice remain in the vessel for another 5 minutes.

Your *Khichdi* should now be ready.

Prep time: 5 minutes

Cooking time: 10 minutes with a pressure cooker; 20-25 minutes with a deep pan

Total time: 15 minutes with a pressure cooker; 25-30 minutes with a deep pan

If using an Instant Pot:

Wash the rice and *dal* together, and let it dry for 5 minutes on an inclined plate.

Turn on the Instant Pot.

Press the Sauté button, and take it to high.

Add the ghee in the inner pot.

When the ghee warms up, add the *Khada Garam Masala* and Asafoetida.

Let these all crackle but NOT burn.

Now add the onion and ginger.

Sauté this for 2 minutes, and then add the peas and the carrots.

Stir well.

Now add the coarsely chopped spinach, turmeric, coriander powder, red chilli powder, and salt.

Add the rice, *dal,* and the tomatoes.

Stir well.

Add the water and close the lid. Press the rice button. Otherwise pressure cook for 5 minutes. And let it cool naturally.

You will find your *Khichdi* ready.

Prep time: 5 minutes

Cooking time: 10 minutes with Instant Pot

Total time: 15 minutes

Note: Different Instant Pot models may have different designs or control options, so please feel free to adapt as you deem fit.

Pongal

INGREDIENTS

Rice-3/4 cup (approx. 150 grams or 5 oz.)

Moong Dal (Split Bengal Gram)-1/4 cup (approx. 50 grams or 1.75 oz.)

Ginger-1 inch (2.5 cm or 1/3rd length of a finger) piece

Turmeric (*Haldi*)-1 teaspoon

Asafoetida (*Hing*)-1/4 teaspoon

Ghee (clarified butter)-2 tablespoon full

Salt- 1 level teaspoon roughly or to taste.

Water-3 cups

Method

Wash the rice and *dal* together and let it dry for 5 minutes on an inclined plate.

If using a pressure cooker:

In a pressure cooker, put the clarified butter, and put it on your heat source.

As it warms up, add the Asafoetida (*Hing*) and ginger.

Let this brown but NOT burn.

Now add the rice, *dal*, turmeric, and the salt.

Stir well.

Add the water, and put the lid with the weight on the cooker.

After the cooker comes to full pressure (don't worry, you will hear that typical sound), switch off the heat source, but do NOT release the pressure.

Let the pressure cooker cool down by itself.

Open the cooker, and you will find your *Pongal* ready.

If using a thick bottomed pan/vessel:

In a pan/vessel, add the clarified butter, and place it on your heat source.

When the butter warms up, add the Asafoetida (*Hing*) and ginger.

Let this brown but NOT burn.

Now add the rice, *dal*, turmeric, and the salt.

Stir well.

Add the water.

Cover the pan/vessel with a well-fitting lid.

Reduce the heat to minimum. In other words, if cooking on gas, turn the knob to SIM (mer). Let the *Pongal* cook for 15-20 minutes.

Switch off the heat source, and let the rice remain in the vessel for another 5 minutes.

Your *Pongal* should now be ready.

Prep time: 5 minutes

Cooking time: 10 minutes with a pressure cooker; 20-25 minutes with a deep pan

Total time: 15 minutes with a pressure cooker; 25-30 minutes with a deep pan

If using an Instant Pot:

Wash the rice and *dal* together, and let it dry for 5 minutes on an inclined plate.

Turn on the Instant Pot.

Press the Sauté button, and take it to high.

Add ghee in the inner pot.

When the ghee warms up, add the Asafoetida (*Hing*) and ginger.

Let this brown but NOT burn.

Now add the rice, *dal*, turmeric, and the salt.

Stir well.

Add the water. Close the lid and press the rice button. Otherwise pressure cook for 5 minutes. And let it cool naturally.

You will find your *Pongal* ready.

Prep time: 5 minutes

Cooking time: 10 minutes with Instant Pot

Total time: 15 minutes

Note: Different Instant Pot models may have different designs or control options, so please feel free to adapt as you deem fit.

Sweet Pongal

INGREDIENTS

Rice-3/4 cup (approx. 150 grams or 5 oz.)

Moong Dal (Split Bengal Gram)-1/4 cup (approx. 50 grams or 1.75 oz.)

Jaggery (*Gur* which is unprocessed sugar)-1 cup (approx. 200 grams or 7 oz.)

Roasted Cashew nuts-2 tablespoon (fried golden and then chopped up.

The method to fry the cashew nuts: in a small pan, add about a tablespoon of cooking oil. Put the pan on your heat source. When the oil heats up, add the cashew nuts, and stir till they turn golden. Immediately remove the cashew nuts to a plate and chop. Remember, if you leave the cashew nuts in the pan, the hot oil will keep roasting the cashew nuts and burn them.

Ghee (clarified butter)-2 tablespoon

Water-3 cups

Method

Wash the rice and *dal* together, and let it dry for 5 minutes on an inclined plate.

If using a pressure cooker:

In a pressure cooker, put the clarified butter and put it on your heat source.

As it warms up, add the rice and lentils.

Stir well.

Add 2 cups of water, and put the lid with the weight on the cooker.

After the cooker comes to full pressure (don't worry, you will hear that typical sound), switch off the heat source, but do NOT release the pressure.

Let the pressure cooker cool down by itself.

Meanwhile, in a pan melt the jaggery with 1 cup water, and let it come to a boil.

Open the cooker, and add the boiled jaggery to it along with the roasted cashew nuts.

Mix well.

Your Sweet *Pongal* is ready.

If using a thick bottomed pan/vessel:

In a pan/vessel, add the clarified butter, and place it on your heat source.

When the butter warms up, add the rice and lentil.

Stir well.

Add 2 cups of water.

Cover the pan/vessel with a well-fitting lid.

Reduce the heat to minimum.

In other words, if cooking on gas, turn the knob to SIM (mer). Let the *Pongal* cook for 15-20 minutes.

Switch off the heat source and let the rice remain in the vessel for another 5 minutes.

Meanwhile, in a pan melt the jaggery with 1 cup water, and let it come to a boil.

Open the cooker, and add the boiled jaggery to it along with the roasted cashew nuts.

Mix well.

Your Sweet *Pongal* is ready.

Prep time: 5 minutes

Cooking time: 10 minutes with a pressure cooker; 20-25 minutes with a deep pan

Total time: 15 minutes with a pressure cooker; 25-30 minutes with a deep pan

If using an Instant Pot:

Wash the rice and *dal* together, and let it dry for 5 minutes on an inclined plate.

Turn on the Instant Pot.

Press the Sauté button, and take it to high.

Add ghee in the inner pot.

When the ghee warms up, add the rice and lentils.

Stir well.

Add 2 cups of water. Close the lid and press the rice button. Otherwise pressure cook for 5 minutes. And let it cool naturally.

Meanwhile, in a pan melt the jaggery with 1 cup water, and let it come to a boil.

Open the Instant Pot, and press the Sauté button.

Add the boiled jaggery to it along with the roasted cashew nuts.

Mix well.

Your Sweet *Pongal* is ready.

Prep time: 5 minutes

Cooking time: 10 minutes with Instant Pot

Total time: 15 minutes

Note: Different Instant Pot models may have different designs or control options, so please feel free to adapt as you deem fit.

Idlis (Steamed rice and lentil cakes)

INGREDIENTS

Dhuli Urad dal (Split and de-husked Black Lentils) -1/2 cup (approx. 100 grams or 3.5 oz.)

Rice flour-1 cup (approx. 200 grams or 7 oz.)

(The ratio of dal:rice here is suggested to be 1:2 so as to increase the protein content of this dish. You can, however, increase this ratio to 1:3 or even 1:4 if you want your idlis to be as soft as in restaurants in India.)

Poha (flattened rice) - 1 tablespoon (or Fenugreek seeds – ½ teaspoon)

Baking powder-1 level teaspoon

Salt– 1/2 tea spoon or to taste

Cooking Oil/Clarified butter for greasing the *idli* mould

Method

Soak the *urad dal* (with Fenugreek seeds, if you are using them) for at least 4 hours, and then make it into a fine paste in a blender.

Add the rice flour, *poha* (if you are NOT using Fenugreek seeds), and some water to make a thick batter and blend again.

Pour this mixture into a vessel and let it ferment (that is let the batter puff up) for the next 12 to 24 hours, depending on what the ambient temperatures are. If it is too cold, then wait for 24 hours and go ahead.

Before steaming the *idlis*, add the salt, and baking powder.

Grease the *idli* stand, and then pour a tablespoon of the idli batter into each mould.

If using pressure cooker, add water in the cooker which comes below the last mould.

Place the *idli* stand in the cooker.

Close the lid **without the weight**.

Light the heat source, and place your cooker on it.

When steam starts coming out, reduce the heat (to SIM on a gas stove), and cook for about 10-15 minutes, or till the *idlis* become firm and can be easily taken out of the mould.

Switch off the heat source.

Remove the *idli* stand from the water and gently nudge out the *idlis* onto a serving plate.

The *idlis* taste excellent with *sambar* (recipe in Chapter 3) and coconut chutney (recipe in Chapter 4).

Prep time: Overnight (for soaking, grinding, and mixing the *idli batter*)

Cooking time: 15 minutes

Total time: Overnight + 15 minutes

Dosa

INGREDIENTS

Dhuli Urad dal (Split and de-husked Black Lentils) -1 cup (approx. 200 grams or 7 oz.)

Chana Dal (Split Chickpea) – 2 tablespoons

Methi (Fenugreek) seeds – 1 teaspoon

Rice flour-2 cups (approx. 400 grams or 14 oz.)

Salt– 1/2 tea spoon or to taste

Baking Powder- 1 teaspoon

Cooking Oil/Butter-1 tablespoon per *dosa*

Method

Soak the *Urad Dal, Chana Dal, and Methi seeds* in two cups of water over night or for at least six hours.

Take out the soaked *dals* from the water, put it in a blender, and blend well using some water BUT DO NOT LET IT BECOME TOO WATERY.

The batter should feel absolutely smooth to the touch.

In this mixture, add the rice flour and some water, and switch on the blender again to turn this all into a thick batter which has a pouring consistency.

Pour the mixture into a suitable vessel, cover it and let it ferment (that is let the batter puff up) for the next 12 to 24 hours, depending on what the ambient temperatures are.

Add the salt and baking powder, when you are ready to cook.

In a large non-stick girdle, spread about half a cup of batter evenly.

Put it on your heat source.

Let the *dosa* cook.

Add the oil on the top side and a little on the corners.

Do not disturb the *dosa* till it starts browning.

You can then gently nudge the *dosa* at the edge, and it will come out on its own when it is done.

Remove the *dosa* to a plate.

It is greater fun if you can eat it right away, with some *masala* filling and coconut *chutney* (recipe in Chapter 4).

Add *sambar* (recipe in Chapter 3) too for a full authentic South Indian experience.

For the next *dosa*, you will need to cool down the girdle OTHERWISE YOU WILL NOT BE ABLE TO SPREAD THE BATTER.

To do so, therefore, wash the girdle in cold water, and follow the above mentioned method again.

Prep time: Overnight (for soaking, grinding, and mixing the *dosa batter*)

Cooking time: 15 minutes

Total time: Overnight + 15 minutes

Chapter 3: Lentils as Snacks and Accompaniments

LENTILS VERY EASILY lend themselves for savory snacks and accompaniments. *Dosas* and *Idlis* (recipes in Chapter 2) are popular, especially in South India. In North India, however, it will generally be some kind of hot *Pakoras* that will accost your cup of steaming tea, especially on a cool rainy day.

Pakoras (Vegetable Fritters)

VEGETABLE FRITTERS are popular snacks to be eaten any time of the day, with any kind of drink. All kinds of vegetables can be used for this tasty snack. We present some seven of the most popular ones.

Please note that most pakoras look like fried dumplings whether you make it of onions, spinach, cauliflower, potato, or bottle gourd.

Onion Pakoras

INGREDIENTS

Chickpea flour-1 cup (approx. 200 grams or 7 oz.)

Rice flour-1/2 cup (approx. 100 grams or 3.5 oz.)

Baking powder-1/2 teaspoon

Asafoetida (*Hing*)-1/2 teaspoon

Coriander powder-1 teaspoon

Cumin seeds (*Jeera*)-1/2 teaspoon

Turmeric (*Haldi*)-1/2 teaspoon

Red Chilli powder-1/2 teaspoon (just for flavor and not to make it hot; you can add more if you like it hot)

Salt– 1/2 tea spoon or to taste

Water-1 cup (approximately)

Sliced Onions-4

Oil for deep frying

Method

Mix all the ingredients well, except the onions.

Add the water and beat until smooth and light.

It should be of a thin coating consistency.

Set it aside for at least 15 minutes. This helps the flour to absorb the water well and attain a thicker consistency.

If it becomes too thick, you may add a little more water, and beat well.

Add the onions to this batter.

Heat oil in a frying pan or wok.

Take the mixture with the onion slices, a tablespoonful at a time, and drop into the hot oil.

Be careful of the splatter that follows.

You will find that the fritters swell up.

Gently turn them around, and take out from the oil when they are nice and golden brown.

Remove to a dish, which is covered with a paper napkin, so that all the excess oil can be absorbed.

Repeat till all the fritters/*pakoras* are fried.

Enjoy with any of the *chutneys*, especially the mint *chutney*.

Prep time: 20 minutes

Cooking time: 3 minutes @ each batch

Total time: Approximately 30 minutes

Paneer Pakoras (Cottage Cheese fritters)

INGREDIENTS

Chickpea flour-1 cup (approx. 200 grams or 7 oz.)

Rice flour-1/2 cup (approx. 100 grams or 3.5 oz.)

Baking powder-1/2 teaspoon

Asafoetida (*Hing*)-1/2 teaspoon

Coriander powder-1 teaspoon

Cumin seeds (*Jeera*)-1/2 teaspoon

Turmeric (*Haldi*)-1/2 teaspoon

Red Chilli powder-1/2 teaspoon (just for flavor and not to make it hot; you can add more if you like it hot)

Salt– 1/2 tea spoon or to taste

Water-1 cup (approximately)

Paneer (Cottage Cheese)-300 grams (10 oz or 1 cup)

Oil for deep frying

Method

Mix all the ingredients well, except the *paneer*.

Add the water and beat until smooth and light.

It should be of a thin coating consistency.

Set it aside for at least 15 minutes. This helps the flour to absorb the water well and attain a thicker consistency.

If it becomes too thick, you may add a little more water and beat well.

Slice the *paneer* into bite size pieces, and add to the batter.

Heat oil in a frying pan or wok.

Take the mixture with the *paneer* a tablespoonful at a time, and drop into the hot oil.

Be careful of the splatter that follows.

You will find that the fritters swell up.

Gently turn them around, and take out from the oil when they are nice and golden brown.

Remove to a dish, which is covered with a paper napkin, so that all the excess oil can be absorbed.

Repeat till all the fritters/*pakoras* are fried.

Enjoy with any of the chutneys.

Prep time: 20 minutes

Cooking time: 3 minutes @ each batch

Total time: Approximately 30 minutes

Palak Pakoras (Spinach fritters)

INGREDIENTS

Chickpea flour-1 cup (approx. 200 grams or 7 oz.)

Rice flour-1/2 cup (approx. 100 grams or 3.5 oz.)

Baking powder-1/2 teaspoon

Asafoetida (*Hing*)-1/2 teaspoon

Coriander powder-1 teaspoon

Cumin seeds (*Jeera*)-1/2 teaspoon

Turmeric (*Haldi*)-1/2 teaspoon

Red Chilli powder-1/2 teaspoon (just for flavor and not to make it hot; you can add more if you like it hot)

Salt– 1/2 tea spoon or to taste

Water-1 cup (approximately)

Spinach (only leaves)-300 grams (10oz or 2 cups)

Oil for deep frying

Method

Mix all the ingredients, except the spinach, well.

Add the water and beat until smooth and light.

It should be of a thin coating consistency.

Set it aside for at least 15 minutes. This helps the flour to absorb the water well and attain a thicker consistency.

If it becomes too thick, you may add a little more water and beat well.

Add the spinach to this batter.

Heat oil in a frying pan or wok.

Take the mixture with the spinach, a leaf at a time, and drop into the hot oil.

Be careful of the splatter that follows.

You will find that the fritters swell up.

Gently turn them around, and take out from the oil when they are nice and golden brown.

Remove to a dish, which is covered with a paper napkin, so that all the excess oil can be absorbed.

Repeat till all the fritters/*pakoras* are fried.

Enjoy with any of the *chutneys*.

Prep time: 20 minutes

Cooking time: 3 minutes @ each batch

Total time: Approximately 30 minutes

Gobi Pakoras (Cauliflower Fritters)

INGREDIENTS

Chickpea flour-1 cup (approx. 200 grams or 7 oz.)

Rice flour-1/2 cup (approx. 100 grams or 3.5 oz.)

Baking powder-1/2 teaspoon

Asafoetida (*Hing*)-1/2 teaspoon

Coriander powder-1 teaspoon

Cumin seeds (*Jeera*)-1/2 teaspoon

Turmeric (*Haldi*)-1/2 teaspoon

Red Chilli powder-1/2 teaspoon (just for flavor and not to make it hot; you can add more if you like it hot)

Salt– 1/2 tea spoon or to taste

Water-1 cup (approximately)

Cauliflower-1 (with florets separated into bite size)

Oil for deep frying

Method

Mix all the ingredients, except the cauliflower, well.

Add the water and beat until smooth and light.

It should be of a thin coating consistency.

Set it aside for at least 15 minutes. This helps the flour to absorb the water well and attain a thicker consistency.

If it becomes too thick, you may add a little more water and beat well.

Add the cauliflower to this batter.

Heat oil in a frying pan or wok.

Take the mixture with the cauliflower, a tablespoonful at a time, and drop into the hot oil.

Be careful of the splatter that follows.

You will find that the fritters swell up.

Gently turn them around, and take out from the oil when they are nice and golden brown.

Remove to a dish, which is covered with a paper napkin, so that all the excess oil can be absorbed.

Repeat till all the fritters/*pakoras* are fried.

Enjoy with any of the *chutneys*.

Prep time: 20 minutes

Cooking time: 3 minutes @ each batch

Total time: Approximately 30 minutes

Baingan Pakoras (Aubergine Fritters)

INGREDIENTS

Chickpea flour-1 cup (approx. 200 grams or 7 oz.)

Rice flour-1/2 cup (approx. 100 grams or 3.5 oz.)

Baking powder-1/2 teaspoon

Asafoetida (*Hing*)-1/2 teaspoon

Coriander powder-1 teaspoon

Cumin seeds (*Jeera*)-1/2 teaspoon

Turmeric (*Haldi*)-1/2 teaspoon

Red Chilli powder-1/2 teaspoon (just for flavor and not to make it hot; you can add more if you like it hot)

Salt– 1/2 tea spoon or to taste

Water-1 cup (approximately)

Round big Aubergines-2 (thinly sliced)

Oil for deep frying

Method

Mix all the ingredients, except the aubergines, well.

Add the water and beat until smooth and light.

It should be of a thin coating consistency.

Set it aside for at least 15 minutes. This helps the flour to absorb the water well and attain a thicker consistency.

If it becomes too thick, you may add a little more water and beat well.

Add the aubergine slices to this batter.

Heat oil in a frying pan or wok.

Take the mixture with the aubergines, a slice at a time, and drop into the hot oil.

Be careful of the splatter that follows.

You will find that the fritters swell up.

Gently turn them around and take out from the oil when they are nice and golden brown.

Remove to a dish, which is covered with a paper napkin, so that all the excess oil can be absorbed.

Repeat till all the fritters/*pakoras* are fried.

Enjoy with any of the *chutneys*.

Prep time: 20 minutes

Cooking time: 3 minutes @ each batch

Total time: Approximately 30 minutes

Aloo Pakoras (Potato Fritters)

INGREDIENTS

Chickpea flour-1 cup (approx. 200 grams or 7 oz.)

Rice flour-1/2 cup (approx. 100 grams or 3.5 oz.)

Baking powder-1/2 teaspoon

Asafoetida (*Hing*)-1/2 teaspoon

Coriander powder-1 teaspoon

Cumin seeds (*Jeera*)-1/2 teaspoon

Turmeric (*Haldi*)-1/2 teaspoon

Red Chilli powder-1/2 teaspoon (just for flavor and not to make it hot; you can add more if you like it hot)

Salt– 1/2 tea spoon or to taste

Water-1 cup (approximately)

Potatoes-4 (thinly sliced)

Oil for deep frying

Method

Mix all the ingredients, except the potatoes, well.

Add the water and beat until smooth and light.

It should be of a thin coating consistency.

Set it aside for at least 15 minutes. This helps the flour to absorb the water well and attain a thicker consistency.

If it becomes too thick, you may add a little more water and beat well.

Add the potato slices to this batter.

Heat oil in a frying pan or wok.

Take the mixture with the potatoes, a slice at a time, and drop into the hot oil.

Be careful of the splatter that follows.

You will find that the fritters swell up.

Gently turn them around, and take out from the oil when they are nice and golden brown.

Remove to a dish, which is covered with a paper napkin, so that all the excess oil can be absorbed.

Repeat till all the fritters/*pakoras* are fried.

Enjoy with any of the *chutneys*.

Prep time: 20 minutes

Cooking time: 3 minutes @ each batch

Total time: Approximately 30 minutes

Lauki Pakoras (Bottle Gourd Fritters)

INGREDIENTS

Chickpea flour-1 cup (approx. 200 grams or 7 oz.)

Rice flour-1/2 cup (approx. 100 grams or 3.5 oz.)

Baking powder-1/2 teaspoon

Asafoetida (*Hing*)-1/2 teaspoon

Coriander powder-1 teaspoon

Cumin seeds (*Jeera*)-1/2 teaspoon

Turmeric (*Haldi*)-1/2 teaspoon

Red Chilli powder-1/2 teaspoon (just for flavor and not to make it hot; you can add more if you like it hot)

Salt– 1/2 tea spoon or to taste

Water-1 cup (approximately)

Lauki (Bottle Gourd)-1 (thinly sliced)

Oil for deep frying

Method

Mix all the ingredients, except the bottle gourd, well.

Add the water and beat until smooth and light.

It should be of a thin coating consistency.

Set it aside for at least 15 minutes. This helps the flour to absorb the water well and attain a thicker consistency.

If it becomes too thick, you may add a little more water and beat well.

Add the gourd to this batter.

Heat oil in a frying pan or wok.

Take the mixture with the gourd, a slice at a time, and drop into the hot oil.

Be careful of the splatter that follows.

You will find that the fritters swell up.

Gently turn them around, and take out from the oil when they are nice and golden brown.

Remove to a dish, which is covered with a paper napkin, so that all the excess oil can be absorbed.

Repeat till all the fritters/*pakoras* are fried.

Enjoy with any of the *chutneys*.

Prep time: 20 minutes

Cooking time: 3 minutes @ each batch

Total time: Approximately 30 minutes

Vadas (Fried Lentil Cakes)

INGREDIENTS

Urad dal dhuli (Split and de-husked Black Lentils) - 1 cup (approx. 200 grams or 7 oz.)

Baking powder-1 level teaspoon

Asafoetida (*Hing*) - ½ tea spoon

Crushed Ginger (fresh) - 1 tea spoon

Cumin seed powder- ½ tea spoon

Salt– 1/2 tea spoon or to taste

Cooking Oil for deep frying

Method

Soak the *urad dal* for at least 4 hours.

Put this in a blender/heavy duty kitchen machine along with all other ingredients, except the oil, and make into a fine paste.

Remember to add only a tablespoon or two of water to facilitate blending.

If you add too much water, your *vadas* will simply disintegrate in the oil while frying.

Now heat oil in a small wok.

Since you are deep frying, your wok should be half full with oil.

Keep water in a vessel and dip your hands in it to wet both your hands.

Take a table spoon of the paste in your hands, and make a small hole in the middle with your finger.

Gently slide this into the oil ensuring that you don't touch the hot oil.

As the *vada* cooks on one side, gently flip it to cook on the other side.

Depending on the size of your wok, you should fry not more than 2-3 *vadas* at a time.

When the *vadas* become golden, take them out of the oil, and put them on a plate lined with a paper napkin to absorb the excess oil.

Enjoy with *sambar* (recipe in Chapter 3) and coconut chutney (recipe in Chapter 4).

Preparation Time: 7 minutes (after pre-soaking)

Cooking Time: @2 minutes per *vada*; about 20 minutes for ten *vadas*.

Total Time: 27 minutes

Maddur Vadas (Fried Chickpea Lentil Cakes)

INGREDIENTS

Chana dal (Spilt Chickpea) - 1 cup (approx. 200 grams or 7 oz.)

Baking powder-1 level teaspoon

Asafoetida (*Hing*) - ½ tea spoon

Deseeded Green Chillies- 1 (chopped) (just for flavor and not to make it hot; you can use the seeds if you like it hot)

Onion- 1 (chopped)

Cumin seed - ½ tea spoon

Curry Leaves- a few (10-12)

Salt-1/2 teaspoon (or to taste)

Cooking Oil for deep frying

Method

Soak the *Chana dal* for at least 4 hours.

Put this in a blender/heavy duty kitchen machine and make into a coarse paste.

Take this out in a bowl, and add the rest of the ingredients, except the oil.

Mix well.

Now heat oil in a small wok.

Since you are deep frying, your wok should be half full with oil.

Take a table spoon of the paste in your hands, and make it into a small patty.

Gently slide this into the oil ensuring that you don't touch the hot oil.

As the *Maddur Vada* cooks on one side, gently flip it to cook on the other side.

Depending on the size of your wok, you should fry not more than 2-3 *vadas* at a time.

When the *vadas* become golden, take them out of the oil, and put them on a plate lined with a paper napkin to absorb the excess oil.

Enjoy with *sambar* (recipe in Chapter 3) and coconut chutney (recipe in Chapter 4).

Preparation Time: 7 minutes (after pre-soaking)

Cooking Time: @2 minutes per *vada*; about 20 minutes for ten *vadas*.

Total Time: 27 minutes

Dahi Vadas (Fried Lentil Cakes in a Yoghurt Sauce)

INGREDIENTS FOR VADAS

Urad dal dhuli (Split and de-husked Black Lentils) - 1 cup (approx. 200 grams or 7 oz.)

Baking powder-1 level teaspoon

Asafoetida (*Hing*) - ½ tea spoon

Crushed Ginger (fresh) - 1 tea spoon

Cumin seed powder- ½ tea spoon

Salt– 1/2 tea spoon or to taste

Cooking Oil for deep frying

Ingredients for Yoghurt Sauce

Yoghurt-500 grams (approx. 2 cups or 15 oz)

Black Salt-1/4 teaspoon

Cumin seeds (pre-roasted and crushed)-1 teaspoon

Fresh Coriander Leaves- 2 tablespoons (chopped)

Fresh Ginger- 1 tablespoon (chopped)

Deseeded Green Chillies- 1 (chopped) (just for flavor and not to make it hot; you can use the seeds if you like it hot)

Normal salt-1 teaspoon or to taste

Sugar-3 tablespoon

Method for making the Vadas

Soak the *urad dal* for at least 4 hours.

Put this in a blender/heavy duty kitchen machine along with all other ingredients, except the oil, and make into a fine paste.

Remember to add a tablespoon or two of water ONLY to facilitate blending.

If you add too much water, your *vadas* will simply disintegrate in the oil while frying.

Now heat oil in a small wok.

Since you are deep frying, your wok should be half full with oil.

Keep water in a vessel and dip your hands in it to wet both your hands.

Take a table spoon of the paste in your hands, and make a small hole in the middle with your finger.

Gently slide this into the oil ensuring that you don't touch the hot oil.

As the *vada* cooks on one side, gently flip it to cook on the other side.

Depending on the size of your wok, you should fry not more than 2-3 *vadas* at a time.

When the *vadas* become golden, take them out of the oil, and put them in a bowl filled with fresh water.

This will take out the excess oil.

Squeeze the water out of the *vadas* gently, and put it in a deep serving bowl, to be covered with the yoghurt sauce which we will make now.

Method for the yoghurt sauce

In a bowl, whisk the yoghurt well with black salt, normal salt, sugar, and cumin powder.

Pour this over the *vadas* that have been put in the serving bowl.

Sprinkle the coriander, ginger, and green chillies.

That's all.

Your *Dahi Vadas* are ready.

Preparation Time for *vadas*: 7 minutes (after pre-soaking)

Cooking Time: @2 minutes per *vada*; about 20 minutes for ten *vadas*.

Prep time for yoghurt sauce: 5 minutes

Cooking time: Nil

Total time: 32 minutes

Coconut Chutney

INGREDIENTS

Fresh or Dried Coconut-1

Roasted *Chana dal* (Split Chickpea)-1/2 cup (approx. 100 grams or 3.5 oz.)

Onion small-1/2

Garlic-6 cloves

Ginger-1 inch

Green chilli-1 de-seeded (just for flavor and not to make it hot; you can use the seeds if you like it hot)

Clarified Butter (*Ghee*)-1 tablespoon

Black Mustard seeds (*Rai*)-1 teaspoon

Curry leaves-10-12

Salt– 1/2 tea spoon or to taste

Sugar-1/2 teaspoon

Yoghurt-1/2 cup (approx. 100 grams or 3.5 oz.)

Milk-1 cup (approx. 200 ml or 3.5 oz.)

Method

In a blender, blend together the coconut, *dal*, onion, garlic, ginger, and green chilli.

Add the yoghurt.

When the mixture looks like it is a little crushed, and add the salt and the sugar.

Gently add the milk to make a thick batter.

If your chutney is too thick, you can add some more milk till you achieve the desired consistency.

Take out the chutney in a serving dish.

In a tempering pan, add the *ghee*, the black mustard seeds and the curry leaves, and let it all splutter.

Add this to the coconut *chutney*.

In case, you cannot get curry leaves, black mustard seeds alone can also impart the required flavor.

This *chutney* is an excellent accompaniment for *dosa*, *idlis*, and any other South Indian savory.

Prep Time: 7 minutes

Cooking Time: 1 minute just for tempering

Total Time: 8 minutes

Chapter 4: Lentil Kebabs

PLEASE NOTE THAT ALL lentil kebabs look like fried patties whether you make them with spinach, soya, or green peas.

Have you ever seen those mouth-watering *Shami Kebabs* and wondered if they could have been prepared using vegetarian ingredients than mince chicken/meat?

Don't worry I may have a solution.

Do you know that you can use legumes and lentils to prepare a similar looking kebab?

Not only do these kebabs look similar, but they can also deceive you in taste. This means you will not be able to distinguish between a mince chicken/meat kebab and a lentil kebab.

Really? Just read on.

Hara Bhara Kebab (Lush Green Kebab)

INGREDIENTS

Peas-1 cup (approx. 200 grams or 7 oz.)

Chana Dal (Split Chickpea) -1/2 cup (approx. 100 grams or 3.5 oz.) (soaked in water for at least 4 hours)

Chopped Garlic-4 cloves

Chopped Ginger-1 inch

Garam Masala (mixture of common Indian spices)-1/2 teaspoon

Tip: If you can't get ready-made *garam masala* mixture from a nearby Indian store, you can make yours by using 1 black cardamom, 3 green cardamoms, 4 cloves, and 1 inch cinnamon-all ground together for this dish.

Red Chilli Powder-1/4 teaspoon (just for flavor and not to make it hot; you can add more if you like it hot)

Salt– 1/2 tea spoon or to taste

Cooking Oil-2 tablespoon

Method

In a wok, add ½ tablespoon cooking oil, and put it on your heat source.

As soon as the oil becomes warm, add the crushed garlic and ginger, and roast for a minute.

Add the green peas and the soaked *chana dal* (split chickpea) without the water.

Stir well.

Now add the *garam masala*, red chilli powder, and salt to taste.

Reduce the heat, and cover the wok.

Cook till the split chickpea and peas become soft but not overcooked.

Turn off the heat source, and grind the mixture in a grinder.

Make small patties with this mixture, and keep aside.

In a non-stick pan, add the left-over cooking oil, and put it on your heat source.

As soon as the oil becomes hot, add the patties, and gently roast on both sides.

That's all. Your *Hara Bhara* Kebab (Lush Green Kebab) is ready.

Prep time: 5 minutes (in addition to the four hours required for soaking the split chickpeas)

Cooking time: 15 minutes

Total time: 20 minutes

Spinach Kebab

INGREDIENTS

Chopped Spinach-2 cups (approx. 300 grams or 10 oz.)

Chana Dal (Split Chickpea) -1/2 cup (approx. 100 grams or 3.5 oz.) (soaked in water for at least 4 hours)

Chopped Garlic-4 cloves

Chopped Ginger-1 inch

Garam Masala (mixture of common Indian spices)-1/2 teaspoon

Tip: If you can't get ready-made *garam masala* mixture from a nearby Indian store, you can make yours by using 1 black cardamom, 3 green cardamoms, 4 cloves, and 1 inch cinnamon-all ground together for this dish.

Red Chilli Powder-1/4 teaspoon (just for flavor and not to make it hot; you can add more if you like it hot)

Salt– 1/2 tea spoon or to taste

Cooking Oil-2 tablespoon

Method

In a wok, add ½ tablespoon cooking oil, and put it on your heat source.

As soon as the oil becomes warm, add the crushed garlic and ginger, and roast for a minute.

Add the chopped spinach and the soaked *chana dal* (split chickpea) without the water.

Stir well.

Now add the *garam masala*, red chilli powder, and salt to taste.

Reduce the heat, and cover the wok.

Cook till the split chickpea and the spinach become soft but not overcooked.

Turn off the heat source, and grind the mixture in a grinder.

Make small patties with this mixture, and keep aside.

In a non-stick pan, add the left-over cooking oil, and put it on your heat source.

As soon as the oil becomes hot, add the patties, and gently roast on both sides.

That's all. Your Spinach Kebab is ready.

Prep time: 5 minutes (in addition to the four hours required for soaking the split chickpeas)

Cooking time: 15 minutes

Total time: 20 minutes

Soya Kebab

INGREDIENTS

Soya granules-1 cup (approx. 200 grams or 7 oz.) (soaked in water for 15 minutes)

Chana Dal (Split Chickpea) -1/2 cup (approx. 100 grams or 3.5 oz.) (soaked in water for at least 4 hours)

Chopped Garlic-4 cloves

Chopped Ginger-1 inch

Garam Masala (mixture of common Indian spices)-1/2 teaspoon

Tip: If you can't get ready-made *garam masala* mixture from a nearby Indian store, you can make yours by using 1 black cardamom, 3 green cardamoms, 4 cloves, and 1 inch cinnamon-all ground together for this dish.

Red Chilli Powder-1/4 teaspoon (just for flavor and not to make it hot; you can add more if you like it hot)

Salt– 1/2 tea spoon or to taste

Cooking Oil-2 tablespoon

Method

In a wok, add ½ tablespoon cooking oil, and put it on your heat source.

As soon as the oil becomes warm, add the crushed garlic and ginger, and roast for a minute.

Add the soya and the soaked *chana dal* (split chickpea) both without the water.

Stir well.

Now add the *garam masala*, red chilli powder, and salt to taste.

Reduce the heat, and cover the wok.

Cook till the split chickpeas become soft but not overcooked.

Turn off the heat source, and grind the mixture in a grinder.

Make small patties with this mixture, and keep aside.

In a non-stick pan, add the left-over cooking oil, and put it on your heat source.

As soon as the oil becomes hot, add the patties, and gently roast on both sides.

That's all. Your Soya Kebab is ready.

Prep time: 5 minutes (in addition to the four hours required for soaking the split chickpeas)

Cooking time: 15 minutes

Total time: 20 minutes

Chapter 5: Legumes and Lentils Cooked With Whole Wheat

HAVE YOU EVER HEARD about the famous Indian *Paratha*?

These fried breads come in various sizes and shapes and also differ a bit from region to region. In the North Indian states of Punjab and Haryana, they are sometimes stuffed with potato, cauliflower, or radish. In the Eastern Indian state of Bihar, however, there is a tradition of stuffing these *Parathas* with peas, or roasted chickpea flour (also known as *Sattu*), or Split Chickpeas (*Chana Dal*). In the West Indian state of Maharashtra too, there is a tradition of stuffing these with Split Chickpeas (*Chana Dal*), but the addition of jaggery turns this into the famous *Puran Poli*.

We discuss the three most famous Bihari stuffed *Paratha* recipes below.

Dal Bhara Paratha (Parathas stuffed with split chickpea)

INGREDIENTS

For the Paratha

Whole Wheat Flour-3 cups (approx. 600 grams or 21 oz.) (enough for 5 p*arathas*)

Salt-1/2 teaspoon

Cooking Oil-1 tablespoonful

Luke Warm Water-1 cup

Cooking Oil or Clarified Butter (*Ghee*) for roasting the *Parathas*; *Ghee* is preferred if you want the authentic taste.

For the filling

Chana Dal (Split Chickpea)-1/2 cup (approx. 100 grams or 3.5 oz.)

Cooking Oil-1 teaspoon

Cumin seeds-1/2 teaspoon

Finely Chopped Ginger-1/2 teaspoon

Garam Masala powder-1/4 teaspoon

Tip: If you can't get ready-made *garam masala* mixture from a nearby Indian store, you can make yours by using 1 black cardamom, 3 green cardamoms, 4 cloves, and 1 inch cinnamon-all ground together for this dish.

Red Chilli powder-1/4 teaspoon (just for flavor and not to make it hot; you can add more if you like it hot)

Salt– 1/2 tea spoon or to taste

Method

Soak the split chickpeas for at least 4 hours.

In a mixing bowl, mix together the wheat flour, salt and one tablespoon cooking oil.

Now make firm dough by adding the water.

Cover the dough, and leave for ½ an hour.

Meanwhile, in a wok, add the cooking oil, and put it on your heat source.

As soon as the oil becomes warm, add the cumin seeds.

In a few seconds, when the cumin seeds become brown (please ensure that they don't burn), add the chopped ginger.

Now, add the soaked chickpeas **without the water**.

Turn the heat/flame to low and add the salt, *garam masala,* and red chilli powder.

Cover and cook for about 5 minutes till the chickpeas are lightly cooked (but not over cooked).

If you over cook, the chickpeas will become mushy and will not be suitable for filling.

Turn off the heat source, and in a blender, crush the chickpeas to a fine powder.

Now, take large walnut sized dough and roll into a ball.

Flatten this ball into a patty.

In the center of this patty, place a tablespoon of the chickpea mixture.

Close the patty from all sides so that the mixture goes in the middle and is covered with the dough.

Again, flatten the dough gently with your hands giving it a round shape.

Cover this mixture gently with dry flour.

Place the dough on a rolling board and flatten with a rolling pin till it gets a nice round shape.

Please press evenly while rolling out so that the chickpeas remain covered with the dough.

Put a griddle on your heat source.

As soon as the griddle becomes hot, place the *Paratha* on it.

Reduce the heat/flame to medium, and let the *Paratha* cook on one side.

Flip over and let it cook on the other side.

Take a teaspoon of oil/*Ghee* and spread it over the side facing you.

Flip over, and repeat the process till the *Paratha* gets a nice, crisp texture.

Line a casserole with a paper napkin, and place the *Paratha* inside it to keep it hot.

Repeat the process till all the *Parathas* are made.

Prep time: 35 minutes

Cooking time: 5 minutes for 5 *parathas* @1 minute per *paratha*

Total time: 40 minutes

Mattar Bhara Paratha (Parathas Stuffed With Green Peas)

INGREDIENTS

For Paratha

Whole Wheat Flour-3 cups (enough for 5 *Parathas*)

Salt-1/2 teaspoon

Cooking Oil-1 tablespoonful

Luke Warm Water-1 cup

Cooking Oil or Clarified Butter (Ghee) for roasting the *Parathas*; Ghee is preferred if you want the authentic taste.

For the filling:

Fresh green peas-1/2 cup (approx. 100 grams or 3.5 oz.)

Cooking Oil-1 teaspoon

Cumin seeds-1/2 teaspoon

Finely Chopped Ginger-1/2 teaspoon

Garam Masala powder-1/4 teaspoon

Tip: If you can't get ready-made *garam masala* mixture from a nearby Indian store, you can make yours by using 1 black

cardamom, 3 green cardamoms, 4 cloves, and 1 inch cinnamon-all ground together for this dish.

Red Chilli powder-1/4 teaspoon (just for flavor and not to make it hot; you can add more if you like it hot)

Salt– 1/2 tea spoon or to taste

Method

In a mixing bowl, mix together the wheat flour, salt, and one tablespoon cooking oil.

Now make a firm dough by adding the water.

Cover the dough, and leave for ½ an hour.

Meanwhile, in a wok, add the cooking oil (or *Ghee*), and put it on your heat source.

As soon as the oil becomes warm, add the cumin seeds.

In a few seconds, when the cumin seeds become brown (please ensure that they don't burn), add the chopped ginger.

Now, add the green peas **without the water**.

Turn the heat/flame to low, and add the salt, *garam masala,* and red chilli powder.

-Cover and cook for about 3 minutes till the peas are lightly cooked but not over cooked.

If you over cook, the peas will become mushy and will not be suitable for filling.

Turn off the heat source and in a blender, crush the peas to a fine powder.

Now, take a large walnut sized dough, and roll into a ball.

Flatten this ball into a patty.

In the center of this patty, place a tablespoon of the pea mixture.

Close the patty from all sides so that the mixture goes in the middle and is covered with a dough.

Again, flatten the dough gently with your hands giving it a round shape.

Cover this mixture gently with dry flour.

Place the dough on a rolling board, and flatten with a rolling pin till it gets a nice round shape.

Please press evenly while rolling out so that the pea mixture remains covered with the dough.

Put a griddle on your heat source.

As soon as the griddle becomes hot, place the *Paratha* on it.

Reduce the flame to medium, and let the *Paratha* cook on one side.

Flip over, and let it cook on the other side.

Take a teaspoon of oil/*Ghee* and spread over the side facing you.

Flip over and repeat the process till the *Paratha* gets a nice, crisp texture.

Line a casserole with a paper napkin and place the *Paratha* inside it to keep it hot.

Repeat the process till all the *Parathas* are made.

Prep time: 35 minutes

Cooking time: 5 minutes for 5 *Parathas* @1 minute per *Parathas*

Total time: 40 minutes

Sattu Bhara Paratha (Parathas Stuffed With Roasted Chickpea Flour)

INGREDIENTS

For Paratha

Whole Wheat Flour-3 cups (enough for 5 *Parathas*)

Salt-1/2 teaspoon

Cooking Oil-1 tablespoonful

Luke Warm Water-1 cup

Cooking Oil or Clarified Butter (*Ghee*) for roasting the *Parathas*; *Ghee* is preferred if you want the authentic taste.

For the filling

Sattu (roasted chickpea flour)-1/2 cup (approx. 100 grams or 3.5 oz.)

Finely Chopped Onion-1

Fresh Chopped Coriander Leaves-Small bunch

Finely Chopped De-seeded Green Chilli-1 (just for flavor and not to make it hot; you can use the seeds if you like it hot)

Ajwain (Bishop's weed or Carom seeds)-1/4 teaspoon

Mangrela (Black Onion seeds)-1/4 teaspoon

Lemon Juice-1 teaspoon

Cooking Oil-1 tablespoon

Salt– 1/2 tea spoon or to taste

Water-1 tablespoon

Method

In a mixing bowl, mix together the wheat flour, salt, and one tablespoon cooking oil.

Now make a firm dough by adding the water.

Cover the dough, and leave for ½ an hour.

Meanwhile, mix together the *Sattu* and all the ingredients mentioned above. It will generally be dry but if you press it together, it will form a ball.

Now, take a large walnut sized dough, and roll into a ball.

Flatten this ball into a patty.

In the center of this patty, place a small ball of the *Sattu* mixture.

Close the patty from all sides so that the *Sattu* mixture goes in the middle and is covered with the dough.

Again, flatten the dough gently with your hands giving it a round shape.

Cover this mixture gently with dry flour.

Place the dough on a rolling board, and flatten with a rolling pin till it gets a nice round shape.

Please press evenly while rolling out so that the *Sattu* mixture remains covered with dough.

Put a griddle on your heat source.

As soon as the griddle becomes hot, place the *Paratha* on it.

Reduce the flame to medium, and let the *Paratha* cook on one side.

Flip over, and let it cook on the other side.

Take a teaspoon of oil/*Ghee* and spread over the side facing you.

Flip over, and repeat the process till the *Paratha* gets a nice, crisp texture.

Line a casserole with a paper napkin, and place the *Paratha* inside it to keep it hot.

Repeat the process till all the *Parathas* are made.

Prep time: 35 minutes

Cooking time: 5 minutes for 5 *Parathas* @1 minute per *Parathas*

Total time: 40 minutes

Chapter 6: Lentils As Desserts

WE NOW COME TO THE unique Indian tradition of using lentils for desserts and present five outstanding dishes that can be made at home and in a JIFFY.

Besan Halwa (Chickpea Flour Dessert)

THIS DESSERT IS FIT for the gods, literally, and so is offered quite frequently in temples and at homes during religious functions.

Ingredients

Chickpea flour (*Besan*)-1 cup (approx. 200 grams or 7 oz.)

Sugar-1/2 cup (approx. 100 grams or 3.5 oz.)

Clarified butter (Ghee)-1/4 cup (approx. 50 grams or 1.75 oz.)

Milk-1 cup (approx. 200 ml or 7 oz.)

Saffron-few strands (about 10) dissolved in milk

Green Cardomom-2 crushed

Cashew nuts-25 grams (1 oz. or 1 + 1/2 tablespoon)

Raisins-25 grams (1 oz. or 1 + 1/2 tablespoon)

Method

In a wok, add the clarified butter, and put it on your heat source.

As soon as the clarified butter warms up, add the *besan* (Chickpea flour) and cashew nuts, and stir till all become light brown and give off a lovely aroma.

Do please ensure that you don't burn the flour!

Add the sugar, milk along with the saffron, cardamom, and raisins to the flour.

Stir well till the dessert (*halwa*) dries up.

That's all.

Your *Besan Halwa* is ready.

Prep time: 5 minutes

Cooking time: 7 minutes

Total time: 12 minutes

Boondi

INGREDIENTS

Chickpea flour- 1 cup (approx. 200 grams or 7 oz.)

Rice flour- 2 table spoons

Green Cardamom – 5

Baking powder- ½ teaspoon

Saffron strands: few (about 10) dissolved in water

Sugar- 1 cup (approx. 200 grams or 7 oz.)

Water- 1½ cup; ½ cup for making the chickpea flour batter, and 1 cup for making the sugar syrup

Ghee (clarified butter) - 1 cup (approx. 200 grams/ml or 7 oz.)

Method

In a bowl, whisk together the chickpea flour, rice flour, baking powder and ½ cup water, till it gets a pouring consistency.

In case the batter becomes too dry, you may add a little more water.

Let the batter stand for a while.

Meanwhile make the sugar syrup.

In a vessel, add the sugar, water, cardamom pods (whole), and the dissolved saffron.

Put this vessel on your heat source and bring the sugar mixture to a boil.

Reduce the heat, and let the mixture boil for another 5 minutes before switching off the heat source.

In a small wok, add the *ghee,* and put it on your heat source.

When the *ghee* heats up, take a slotted spoon and gently pour the chickpea batter through this while shaking the slotted spoon over the *ghee*. This is to ensure that the batter falls into the hot ghee in small droplets.

Fry the droplets in batches.

As soon as one batch becomes golden brown, take it out of the ghee, and transfer to the vessel containing the sugar syrup.

Fry the entire batter similarly.

That's all. Your sweet *Boondi* is ready.

Have this hot or at room temperature.

Prep time: 15 minutes

Cooking time: 20 minutes

Total time: 35 minutes

Motichoor Laddoo

INGREDIENTS

Chickpea flour- 1 cup (approx. 200 grams or 7 oz.)

Green Cardamom – 5

Baking powder- ½ teaspoon

Saffron strands: few (about 10) dissolved in water

Sugar- 1 cup (approx. 200 grams or 7 oz.)

Water- 1½ cup; ½ cup for making chickpea flour batter and 1 cup for making the sugar syrup

Ghee (clarified butter) - 1 cup (approx. 200 grams/ml or 7 oz.)

Method

In a bowl, whisk together the chickpea flour, baking powder and ½ cup water, till it gets a pouring consistency.

In case the batter becomes too dry, you may add a little more water.

Let the batter stand.

Meanwhile make the sugar syrup.

In a vessel, add the sugar, water, cardamom pods (whole), and the dissolved saffron.

Put this vessel on your heat source, and bring the sugar mixture to a boil.

Reduce the heat, and let the mixture boil for another 5 minutes before switching off the heat source.

In a small wok, add the *ghee,* and put it on your heat source.

When the *ghee* heats up, take a slotted spoon and gently pour the chickpea batter through this while shaking the slotted spoon over the *ghee.* This is to ensure that the batter falls into the hot *ghee* in small droplets.

Fry the droplets in batches.

As soon as one batch becomes golden brown, take it out of the *ghee,* and transfer to the vessel containing the sugar syrup.

Fry the entire batter similarly.

Remove the chickpea droplets from the sugar syrup, and crush it well in a blender/mixie.

Make small walnut sized balls from the crushed *boondi* with your hands and place them on a platter.

That's all. Your *Motichoor Laddoos* are ready.

Prep time: 15 minutes

Cooking time: 20 minutes

Laddoo making time: 10 minutes

Total time: 45 minutes

Moong Dal Halwa (Split Bengal Gram Dessert)

INGREDIENTS

Split Bengal Gram (*Dhuli Moong Dal*) - ½ cup (approx. 100 grams or 3.5 oz.) (washed and soaked in water for at least 4 hours)

Sugar-1/2 cup (approx. 100 grams or 3.5 oz.)

Clarified butter (Ghee)-1/4 cup (approx. 50 grams or 1.75 oz.)

Milk-2 cups (approx. 400ml. or 14 oz.)

Saffron-few strands (about 10) dissolved in milk

Green Cardomom-2 crushed

Cashew nuts-25 grams (1 oz.) (1 + 1/2 tablespoon)

Raisins-25 grams (1 oz.) (1 + 1/2 tablespoon)

Method

In a wok, add the clarified butter, and put it on your heat source.

As soon as the clarified butter warms up, add the soaked Split Bengal Gram (*Dhuli Moong Dal*), and stir till it becomes light brown and gives off a lovely aroma.

Add the sugar, milk along with the saffron, cardamom, cashew nuts, and raisins to the flour.

Stir well till the dessert (*halwa*) dries up.

That's all.

Your Split Bengal Gram (*Moong Dal*) *Halwa* is ready.

Prep time: 5 minutes (excluding soaking time of 4 hours)

Cooking time: 15 minutes

Total time: 20 minutes

Besan Laddoos (Chickpea Flour sweet balls)

INGREDIENTS

Chickpea flour (*Besan*)-1 cup (approx. 200 grams or 7 oz.)

Sugar-1 cup (crushed fine) (approx. 200 grams or 7 oz.)

Clarified butter (*Ghee*)-1 cup (approx. 200 grams/ml or 7 oz.) (melted)

Green Cardomom-2 crushed

Method

In a wok, add the chickpea flour (*Besan*), and put it on your heat source.

Stir well till the chickpea flour (*Besan*) becomes light brown and gives off a lovely aroma.

Do please ensure that you don't burn the flour!

Turn off the heat source, and place the chickpea flour (*Besan*) in a bowl. Add the clarified butter (*ghee*), crushed sugar, and crushed green cardamom, and mix well. Make small walnut sized balls from this mixture with your hands and place them on a platter.

That's all. Your *Besan Laddoos* are ready.

Prep time: 5 minutes

Cooking time: 7 minutes

Laddoo making time: 10 minutes

Total time: 22 minutes

APPENDIX

———

TYPES OF LENTILS COMMONLY used in India

Chana Dal: Bengal grams skin removed

Masoor Dal: Red Lentils split and skin removed

Kabuli Chana: Whole Chickpea

Rajma: Red Kidney Beans

Black Masoor: The Whole Lentils sold as green lentils or brown lentils. This has a greeny brown seed coat.

Arhar Dal: Also known as *Toor Dal*, Red Gram *Dal* or Split Pigeon Chickpeas.

Dhuli Moong: Green Bengal Gram split and de-husked. This has a pale yellow colour.

Urad Dal: Black Gram split and de-husked.

Whole Urad Dal: Whole Black Gram which has not been de-husked.

Besan: Chickpea flour

Excerpt from Home Style Indian Cooking In A Jiffy

CHAPTER 4: WHAT OTHER Strange Things Do You Need To Know About Indian Cuisine?

India is a land of strange sights, sounds, smells, customs, traditions, and of course cuisine. But regardless of where you go in India, you will find some common thread binding its varied culinary traditions together. I underline a few here.

Eating in *Thalis*: Traditionally, Indian food used to be served in *Thalis* (round platters), that is everything, from starters to desserts would be served in one go. That is how it is still done on weddings, or on such special occasions, in many parts of India. The guests usually sit on the floor, cross legged and are served on a banana leaf or on plates made of broad leaves.

Food, if not served in one go in a *Thali*, would be served on your leaf plate in a continuous stream. At the end of it all, the leaf plates along with the food remnants will be fed to the cows, thus earning merit for all concerned. No dishwashing, and the most environmentally benign waste disposal possible—you will have to salute the ancient Indians for thinking of everything!

If you would like to sample a typical North Indian or South Indian *Thali*, do look out for a branch of restaurant chains like

Sagar Ratna, Naivedyam, Rajdhani etc. or ask your local hosts for suggestions, when you are next in India.

No Soup, Dal a distant substitute: As you'd immediately notice, soups don't precede a normal Indian meal. In a multi-cuisine restaurant, if you insist, you may be offered a Western or Chinese soup. Some try to even take out the curry from any yoghurt based Chicken dish and serve its diluted version as Chicken *Shorba* (soup). The British came up with a lentil based Mulligatawny soup, but it still hasn't become mainstream.

India being a tropical country, it was probably not necessary to serve soup in the beginning of a meal to warm you up. It is surprising, however, that even culinary traditions of the colder areas, for example in the Himalayan region of India, too don't serve any soup. *Kashmiris* and *Garhwalis* have all kinds of curries but no soup. The nearest thing to soup that the *Kashmiris* and *Ladakhis* have is their salted tea, but that they have it all-through-the-day and almost never before a meal!

Indian cuisine also doesn't involve boiling its meats and veggies first and then thinking about what to do with the stock thereof. Stock is part and parcel of the Indian curry.

And then you have the formidable variety of *dals* that Indians cook. So who needs soups?

Carbs are central not meats: If you see an Indian eating at a *dhaba*, you will immediately notice that rice and breads would be forming more than 60% of that meal. The balance 40% would be distributed over meats, veggies, and lentils.

Western cuisine will traditionally reverse this proportion in favor of the meats. One reason could be that Europe's prolonged winters, and consequently shorter cultivating season, meant that they could rely less on grains.

Most of the Indian sub-continent, and even the South-East Asian countries had no such constraints. They could easily have two crops, and sometimes even three. Islands like Bali, like many places in South India, could sow and reap paddy whenever they wanted. But the moment you go to the colder areas of China or Central Asia, you will find meat gaining the upper hand.

Now that the world economies have integrated so much that you can choose what you can put in your meal platter, what should one do? If you have too much meat, you may exceed your protein requirement and invite problems like high cholesterol, renal stones, and even Gout. On the other hand, if you have too much of carbs, you could have more calories than your body needs, suffer from protein shortage, become overweight, and could be prone to diabetes.

Why not then balance your carbs with proteins and, as Lord Buddha advised some 2600 years back, follow the MIDDLE PATH?

Curries are compulsory: This is so obvious that you just can't miss it. Anywhere you go and you will find curries dominating the Indian meal platter.

Why is it so? One reason could be the need to have lots of water in a tropical country like India. This curries could meet in a very healthy (you are boiling your water after all, aren't you) and appetizing a manner. The second reason could be that if you are growing so much rice you would need some curry to "wet" it, to make it less sticky and more palatable.

This could be the reason that you have curries in all rice growing regions of the world, even in Thailand, Laos, or Myanmar. On the other hand, the non-rice growing and wheat-eating colder areas of China, Afghanistan and Central Asia rely more on barbeques and didn't have much need for curries.

Sweets and salty dishes can be eaten together: This happens, I suppose, because in the *Thali* style of food service there is no way of stopping what you eat first and then next. Certainly in the perfectly democratic world of the Indian cuisine, when you have access to a bevy of salty, sweet, bitter, sour, and hot dishes, you also have the full freedom to decide what you want to eat, with what and when. So you will often see children soothing their taste buds with a spoonful of the sweet dish, whenever they would have had a taste of something bitter or hot. Then you would have the somewhat strange spectacle of *Gujaratis* eating their desserts first and the main meal later.

In temples, you will often be served *Poori-Kheer* (unleavened Indian fried bread with rice pudding) or *Poori-Halwa* (unleavened Indian fried bread with flour dessert) as *prasadam* (blessings).

Can you think of anyone eating an apple pie with roast chicken (together and not as a separate course) anywhere in the world? I'd certainly love to be educated.

Spices not sprinkled on but cooked with: In Indian cuisine, you don't cook something first and then sprinkle some spices on it to make it somewhat palatable. Spices almost always have to be cooked with the main meal to unleash their full flavors and magic.

Sauces not prepared separately: It is again a very common practice in Western cuisine to boil or bake something first and then to pour on it a tomato or cheese based sauce or flambé it with some wine or such other alcoholic beverage.

In India, only restaurants semi cook their meats and vegetables and prepare some sauces separately; both to be mixed the moment someone asks for a tomato or onion or yoghurt based dish. This is because for restaurants, speed is of utmost essence. So they have to keep ingredients ready in a semi-finished condition for a quick conversion in to whatever dishes the customers demand.

However, "Home Style" (or even *dhaba*) Indian food is made in one go with everything cooked together. The only thing to "finish" a curry dish could be the sprinkling of some Coriander (Cilantro) leaves. Similarly, *dals* are tempered later with *Ghee* (clarified butter) and *Jeera* (Cumin seeds) or *Rai* (black mustard seeds).

But these are not exactly sauces that are prepared first and poured on to a cooked dish.

Taste buds continuously titillated with accompaniments like pickles, chutneys, raita, papad…: Foreigners are aghast at the sheer number of titbits that literally litter a typical Indian *Thali*. So you will have pickles, made from vegetables, fruits, and even fish. Then you have all kinds of *Papadums*, *Baris* or *Tilauris* made from lentils. Added to these would be the home made sauces called *Chutneys* and sweet marmalade like preparations made from some fruits called *Murabbas*. And in North India, how can you forget the yoghurt based *Raitas*?

Once a European friend asked me if these accompaniments didn't "confuse" your taste buds unnecessarily.

Well, to be frank, they do. But Indians love that "confusion", because as I've already mentioned, an ideal Indian meal must have a balance of all tastes—sour, salty, bitter, hot, and sweet.

And the best way to ensure that is by adding accompaniments which are generally readymade (like jams, marmalades and sauces in the West) and don't have to be cooked at the last moment.

Less use of ovens or barbeques: Except in the Northern Indian states like Punjab, where buried-in-the-earth ovens called Tandoor are very popular, there has hardly been any tradition of baking in the mainstream Indian cuisine. Boiling, frying, steaming– is all there but whatever little barbequing and baking is done, appears to have come to India from Persia, Turkey, or the Central Asian regions from where many Muslim rulers of India had come.

Again, I believe, weather played a part here. Europe and many other colder areas of the world had to keep some kind of fire going in their homes all the while to keep them warm. It was a matter of time, therefore, when someone stumbled upon an appliance that could be attached to the fireplace to cook or rather bake things without much supervision. Even the smoke that resulted from such fireplaces was discovered to have the ability to cure, dry, and preserve meats and again mainstream Indian cuisine has no tradition of having such "smoked" meats.

But don't worry. Globalization has ensured that whatever cakes, pies, breads, or pizzas you crave for, you will find it available on the Indian shop shelves today.

Chopsticks can't work, cutlery is optional: Chopsticks don't work with Western cuisine either because for that meats or vegetables have to be cut into chopstick-friendly sizes first. Cutlery too is hardly used when you eat a Burger or a Pizza, especially while walking to your office. But can you avoid cutlery in formal dinners?

Well, in India, even in many 5-star hotels, you have to specifically ask for cutlery in their signature Indian restaurants. In weddings, your *Thali* may contain just one spoon for the dessert, if you are lucky.

Many of my European friends can't imagine how you can pick up rice with your fingers and take it to your mouth without half of it falling on the way. To that, I invite them to come and see how expert South Indians can pick up a curry too from their plates (and not their bowls) with their fingers. It's a sight you must not miss while in India.

Till then, just ask for whatever cutlery you need for your Indian meal. You will at least get a spoon, I promise.

Vegetarian dishes mimic the non-vegetarian taste: This happens all the while in the West with soya sausages mimicking the taste and flavors of pork or chicken sausage, for example.

In India, this mimicking takes place in two ways. First, where the non-vegetarian portions of a dish would just be dropped. For example, the popular mutton *Shami* Kebab would be made exactly with the same ingredients but without the mutton mince. You can't do the same with chicken sausage, after dropping the chicken mince, can you?

In the second, you have totally vegetarian versions which are sometimes more prolific than their non-vegetarian counterparts. For example, the normal non-vegetarian *koftas* would be made either with mutton or chicken mince. But its vegetarian versions, trying to mimic the same texture, flavor and taste, would be made of bottle gourd (*Lauki ke Kofte*), jackfruit (*Kathal ke Kofte*), reduced milk (*Khoya ke Kofte*) or one of the lentils (*Moong dal ke Kofte*).

Anoothi Vishal, a noted food critic, has a "hypothesis that this intriguing strain of cooking originated especially to cater to (such matriarchs) who must have surely been interested enough in the relatively more exotic and intricate non-vegetarian dishes that were being cooked up at home but did not want to give up on their religious/caste injunctions."

Be that as it may, do try these beguiling dishes that try to taste like meat dishes, when you are next in India.

Cinnamon is not used in desserts but, you guessed it, in curries: Do you know that Cinnamon (or the Indian *Dalchini*) is one spice that is used both in Eastern (including Indian) as well as Western cuisines?

Indian cuisine is well known to use a mind-numbing variety of spices (the list is indeed long). I have heard quite a few celebrity chefs boasting how a particular kebab recipe of theirs uses thirty-six (or thirty-nine, I don't remember) spices as ingredients. That would be quite an overkill, in my opinion. I'd definitely not recommend that any casual dabbler in Indian cuisine experiments with more than ten spices in one dish. But, as I said, that's just my personal opinion.

Coming back to Cinnamon, however, I can bet that this would definitely be in that long list of spices that our celebrity chefs use to create their exotic Indian dishes. I am not sure whether any of their remaining 35 or 38 spices would be so definitely used in Western cuisine. I have always wondered, therefore, as to why Cinnamon is one of the few exceptions.

There is no doubt that Cinnamon does impart a lovely flavor to any dish. Who can resist the aroma of a freshly baked Apple Pie, Pumpkin pie or a Cinnamon roll!

This brings me to the next interesting difference that in the West Cinnamon is used for preparing sweet things like desserts and pies. In India, however, it is more used for savory things like curries, as Indians prefer Cardamom or Saffron in their desserts more. Cinnamon in fact occupies a pride of place in the preparation of the Indian *garam masala*, a spice mixture that is commonly used in chicken curry, *pulaos*, *biryanis*, vegetable dishes, or even *rajma* or kidney beans curry. *Kashmiris* put Cinnamon powder in their tea which they call "Kehwa" that is usually served after dinner. Many claim that adding a teaspoon of *Cinnamon* and honey in your morning tea would protect you from common cold and stomach worries.

That's actually an excellent suggestion from my personal experience.

You can cook with yoghurt: Eating yoghurt is, of course, no big deal. Flavored or unflavored, frozen or thawed, plain or fortified with probiotics, made from full cream or skimmed milk– the variety that industrially manufactured yoghurt today comes in is simply mindboggling.

But cooking with yoghurt? You cook with cheese and wine but yoghurt– the question would certainly stump most aficionados of European or American or even Chinese or Thai schools of cooking.

But talk to anyone from any part of India, and you would instantly get a whole list of regional dishes that use yoghurt in quite a "matter-of-fact" way. This is because before tomatoes were brought to India by the Portuguese sometimes in the 16th century, yoghurt was the main ingredient (apart from tamarind and pomegranate seeds) that could add a little sour taste to Indian dishes.

In Kashmir, savor the *wazwan* (a feast usually served on special occasions like weddings) and you'd find the pride of place accorded to *Gushtabbas* (pounded boneless meat balls cooked in yoghurt) or *Yakhni* or *Dhania Kormas* (both containing mutton pieces, with bones, cooked in yoghurt, with different spices).

In western Indian states of Maharashtra or Gujarat, *Kadhi* (made from yoghurt or butter milk with added potato, onions or vegetable fritters) would be omnipresent in all vegetarian platters. Punjabi vegetarians too like a slightly different version of this *Kadhi,* but they actually use copious amounts of yoghurt in their popular drink *Lassi* (basically a yoghurt shake).

The Punjabis (as well as the other North-Indian meat eaters) also like to marinate their chicken and mutton with yoghurt before they put it in their tandoors (earthen ovens) or barbeques, or even curries. Yoghurt in these regions is also supposed to bring in good luck as there is a tradition of NOT leaving your house for any long journey or for an examination/ interview without having at least a spoonful of yoghurt with sugar.

The East, specially the Bengal region, is famous for cooking their fish in yoghurt. Just check out their dishes of *Dahi-Machh* (fish cooked in yoghurt and *garam masala*) or *Dahi-sarson* (fish cooked in a yoghurt-mustard sauce). Their yoghurt dessert *Mishti-doi* (literally sweet yoghurt) or *Bhapa-doi* (steamed yoghurt) is simply out-of-this-world.

The southern regions of India are so fond of yoghurt that they usually end their meals, not with a dessert, but with a savory curd-rice. Yoghurt is also a very important ingredient of the south-Indian coconut chutney that goes well with south-Indian snacks like *Idlis*, *Vadas* and *Dosas*.

Books by Prasenjeet Kumar in the "Cooking In A Jiffy" Series

HOME STYLE INDIAN COOKING IN A JIFFY

HOW TO COOK IN A JIFFY EVEN IF YOU HAVE NEVER BOILED AN EGG BEFORE

HEALTHY COOKING IN A JIFFY: THE COMPLETE NO FAD NO DIET HANDBOOK

HOW TO CREATE A COMPLETE MEAL IN A JIFFY

THE ULTIMATE GUIDE TO COOKING RICE THE INDIAN WAY

THE ULTIMATE GUIDE TO COOKING FISH THE INDIAN WAY

THE ULTIMATE GUIDE TO COOKING CHICKEN THE INDIAN WAY

THE ULTIMATE GUIDE TO COOKING VEGETABLES THE INDIAN WAY

THE ULTIMATE GUIDE TO COOKING DESSERTS THE INDIAN WAY

Fiction by Prasenjeet Kumar

LEGALLY IN LOVE

LOVE KARMA CROSSED

WHEN GANGES MET THE NORTH SEA

YOU CAN'T KILL MY LOVE: A KASHMIR HOLOCAUST LOVE STORY

AUTISTICALLY YOURS

STILL MISSING...

WHEN YOU CAN'T TRUST LOVE

THE ENEMY WITHIN

THE SCEPTIC

Books by Prasenjeet Kumar in the "Quiet Phoenix" Series

CELEBRATING QUIET PEOPLE: UPLIFTING STORIES FOR INTROVERTS AND HIGHLY SENSITIVE PERSONS

QUIET PHOENIX: AN INTROVERT'S GUIDE TO RISING IN CAREER & LIFE

QUIET PHOENIX 2: FROM FAILURE TO FULFILMENT: A MEMOIR OF AN INTROVERTED CHILD

CELEBRATING QUIET LEADERS: UPLIFTING STORIES OF INTROVERTED LEADERS WHO CHANGED HISTORY

CELEBRATING QUIET ARTISTS: STIRRING STORIES OF INTROVERTED ARTISTS THE WORLD CAN'T FORGET

Books by Prasenjeet Kumar in the "Self-Publishing WITHOUT SPENDING A DIME" Series

HOW TO BE AN AUTHOR ENTREPRENEUR WITHOUT SPENDING A DIME

HOW TO TRANSLATE YOUR BOOKS WITHOUT SPENDING A DIME

HOW TO MARKET YOUR BOOKS WITHOUT SPENDING A DIME

HOW TO HAVE A HAPPIER WRITER MINDSET WITHOUT SPENDING A DIME

Books by Arun Kumar and Prasenjeet Kumar

KASHMIR IS FREE

KASHMIR THINKS ITS FREE

Books by Sonali Kumar and Prasenjeet Kumar

THE OUTSIDER'S CURSE

THE OUTSIDER'S TALES

Connect With The Author

FEEL FREE TO WRITE to me anytime at ciaj@cookinginajiffy.com.

I would love to connect with you on Social Media. Join me on:

Facebook:

https://www.facebook.com/cookinginajiffy

Twitter:

https://twitter.com/CookinginaJiffy

Goodreads:

https://www.goodreads.com/prasenjeet

Google Plus:

https://www.google.com/+PrasenjeetKumarAuthor

About The Author

PRASENJEET KUMAR IS the author/co-author of over 32 books in four genres: Fiction, motivational books for introverts (the Quiet Phoenix series), books on Self-Publishing (Self-Publishing WITHOUT SPENDING A DIME series) and cookbooks (Cooking In A Jiffy series). His books (over 60 titles and counting) have been translated into French, German, Italian, Japanese, Spanish, and Portuguese, and sell in over 50 countries.

Prasenjeet is a Law graduate from the University College London (2005-2008), London University and a Philosophy Honours graduate from St. Stephen's College (2002-2005), Delhi University. In addition, he holds a Legal Practice Course (LPC) Diploma from College of Law, Bloomsbury, London, and was for a brief while, a solicitor of England and Wales.

Prasenjeet loves gourmet food, music, films, and travelling. He has already covered twenty-four countries including Canada, China, Denmark, Dubai, Germany, Greece, Hong Kong, Indonesia, Israel, Italy, Jordan, Macau, Malaysia, Mauritius, Montenegro, Sharjah, Spain, Sweden, Switzerland, Thailand, Turkey, UK, Uzbekistan, and the USA.

Prasenjeet is the self-taught designer, writer, editor, and proud owner of the website www.cookinginajiffy.com which he has dedicated to his mother. He also runs another website www.publishwithprasen.com where he shares tips about writing and self-publishing.